C000017328

ISBN 978-0-483-81902-3
PIBN 10737257

Legenda Monastica

AND OTHER POEMS

Legenda Monastica

And Other Poems

WITH A PREFACE BY THE

Rev. G. CONGREVE, M.A.

Of the Society of S. John the Evangelist, Cowley

FIFTH EDITION

A. R. MOWBRAY & CO. Ltd.
London : 28 Margaret Street, Oxford Circus, W.
Oxford : 9 High Street
1915

THIS BOOK

IS DEDICATED

WITH AFFECTION AND REVERENCE

TO THE MEMORY OF

THE REV. CANON THOMAS CHAMBERLAIN

FOUNDER OF THE COMMUNITY

OF S. THOMAS-YE-MARTYR

OXFORD

PREFACE

THIS little Book of Monastic Tales, of various origin, in verse, has been a delight to many of us for years.

To some, who to-day are grown old in monastic service, it perhaps gave their first suggestion of the beauty of the cloister, and the joy of virtue won for love by discipline.

As the literary child of a Religious Community, the book, no doubt, had its influence upon the first fervour of the young society in which it was born. It was immediately intended moreover as a pious effort to raise funds for the support of the Orphanage founded by the Sisters of S. Thomas the Martyr in Oxford.

The reader of these traditional stories, that touch with human interest the monastic virtues of Simplicity, Obedience, Punctuality, Diligence, Brotherly Love, Humility, and the Love of GOD, will recognize perhaps a tone of literary fervour that belonged to a particular moment, the early days of the Oxford Revival in the Church of England. It was influenced doubtless by the Christian hymns and ballads of Bishop Coxe of the United States, and of our own Dr. Neale of East Grinstead.

As we read we find that some of the verses attain real literary value, while all are more or less touched with the fire of the Love of GOD, of mankind, and of nature.

I am happy to be allowed to welcome a new edition of the little book which proved a store of jewels for us of the generation that is passing away.

GEORGE CONGREVE.

NOTE :—The Community of S. Thomas the Martyr wish to express their gratitude to Miss Yonge and Father Waggett, S.S.J.E., for their poems, which have hitherto only appeared in periodicals; and also to Messrs. Kegan Paul, Trench, Trübner & Co. Ltd. for permission to reprint a poem by the late Henry Kingsley.

If they have unwittingly infringed the copyright of the verses entitled "Be comforted," they offer their apologies.

Contents

Miscellaneous Poems

Mission Poems and Ballads

Hymns

Legenda Monastica

❧❧❧

'TIS Easter-tide, and earth her LORD to greet
  (Her LORD the Gardener) hath her
  offerings meet.
Her fairest forms, her softest tints, she brings,
Her sweetest songs she now most sweetly
  sings:
Not Summer's richer colouring is here,
But delicate hues from Spring's light hand
  appear;
And from all Nature's voice ascend on high
Low Alleluias, floating to the sky.
Within S. Dunstan's holy house this day
The Brethren seven are met; not ours to say
The look of Heavenly joy, that from each
  face
Yet could not quite Lent's iron mark efface:

Lent whose long vigils and whose Fast and
 Prayer
Have left on all some trace of thought and
 care,
Have in the old more deeply carved deep lines,
And on each novice laid some chastening
 signs;
Thus sobering (like the veil by Moses worn)
The else too dazzling joy of Easter-Morn.
They gather round; and each, with loving gaze,
Smiles on his Brethren, whom for many days
He scarce hath communed with, nor looked
 upon,
Spending his being on his LORD alone.
But none are eager, 'mid that loving throng,
To break the silence, which has been so long
Unto them all as a companion wise,
That they have learnt its calm restraint to
 prize;
Save that one, ever and anon, will cry
Exultingly, and yet half doubtingly,
(As if, in sight of Calvary and the Tomb,
His heart for such strange joy can scarce find
 room,)
"The LORD is Risen!" when swift response is
 heard,

"And unto Simon Peter hath appeared."
The aged Abbot spake, "My sons, I pray,
"That we, whose tongues are loosed this Holy
    Day,
"May only speak what GOD can well approve,
"And build each other up in Heavenly love.
"And to this end, I think, it will be well
"That each in turn unto the rest shall tell
"Some holy legend of the days gone by,
"How Saints o'er sin have won the victory:
"Bring from the treasure-house things new
    and old,
"Tell of the love more precious far than gold,
"Tell of the might of Prayer, how it hath power
"To slake the fierceness of temptation's hour.
"Weave we a festal wreath these Easter
    hours,
"Formed for GOD's honour, and its glorious
    flowers,
"The supernatural graces He hath given
"To those courageous souls who fight for
    Heaven.
"(GOD grant that we His priceless gifts may
    win !)
"You, Brother Wilfrith, shall the round
    begin :

"And after Nones, ere Vesper-hour draws nigh,
"Shall tell a story of 'Simplicity.'"
Wilfrith, the youngest Brother of the House,
Had scarce known eighteen summers; on his
  brows
Few marks of care were seen, and he was
  known
To all the elder Brethren as a son:
A son beloved, indulged it may be too,
For Nature craves such pleasant work to do.
The Abbot, ever with young Brethren stern,
(Lest they should fail of discipline to learn,)
Was harshest—so the Brethren softly said—
With Brother Wilfrith. It may be he read
In that bright face, and in those wondrous eyes,
Which ever took one with a new surprise
At their great beauty—that the boy must feel
The discipline he knew so well to deal.
Perchance he saw how strongly Nature beat
In that young heart, and how surpassing sweet
Was every touch of human love; and how
At but a word of praise, to that bright brow
Would mount the flush of joy; and, it may be,
The old man feared that all too easily,
And counting not the cost, had Wilfrith come
To make that holy House his life-long home.

Whate'er the cause, the youthful novice heard
From the stern Abbot's lips no tender word,
And harder penance followed Wilfrith's falls
Than any other Brother's in those walls.
But still the boy was happy, still he smiled,
And well the Brethren loved the almost child.
Now with his hands crossed meekly on his
 breast,
Blushing he bowed assent to the behest.
" You, Brother Jerome, shall go on from thence
" To praise the glory of Obedience.
" And Brother Gregory shall fitly tell
" How Punctuality avails us well."
And thus to each, in accents grave and kind,
The holy man a varying theme assigned.
And here the wreath they wove that Easter
 time,
Of quaint old stories clad in uncouth rhyme,
Is brought to light; nor may we read with
 scorn—
Albeit enlightened days our lives adorn—
The simple tale of graces prized of old
That in dark days remote these Brethren told.

BROTHER WILFRITH'S STORY.

SIMPLICITY.

LONG years ago, ere Convents rose, as now
    to GOD they rise,
The ladders framed like Jacob's whereby man
    may scale the skies,
Seven holy men, to JESUS drawn by cords of
    Heavenly love,
Resolved to live below the life that angels
    live above;
To GOD their lives to dedicate, and pray by
    day and night,
To serve Him with unswerving love, and
    'gainst His foes to fight.
But poor these men, yea, poor and old, they
    laboured for their bread,
Dwelt meanly,—like to Him Who had not
    where to lay His Head,—

And for their Chapel, whence should rise
    seven times a day their praise,
They chose a lovely forest glade that caught
    the sun's first rays.
It was a Chapel such as never House can
    boast this day,
And thro' the clustering arches green the
    sunbeams loved to stray;
And in the East an Altar there they raised
    with reverent care,
And hourly from that fane arose the voice
    of praise and prayer.
One grief they had: they could not sing,
    their voices all were gone,
Besides they knew no hymn, nor chant, nor
    any simple tone.
The Abbot then decreed that since GOD
    knew they could not sing,
He would accept it if they brought the best
    they had to bring.
"So we will simply say our hymns, excepting
    one, and that,
"The Hymn of Holy Mary Maid, the glad
    Magnificat.
"We all, my sons, must try and chant, and
    CHRIST in Heaven above,

"If all our music is but harsh, will look
      upon our love."
So day by day at Vesper time *Magnificat*
      was heard ;
'Tis said that from the boughs above it
      frightened every bird ;
For all were out of tune, and each a different
      chant would try ;
But up in heaven, where hearts are known,
      it made sweet melody.
On Christmas Eve, 'mid cold and snow,
      a youth came to their door,
Praying that he that brotherhood might join
      for evermore.
'Twas Vesper time and straightway then his
      voice arose in praise
'Twas as a seraph's voice ; the brethren
      listened in amaze,
And each one in his heart exclaimed, "Thank
      GOD that on this night
"One is among us who can sing *Magnificat*
      aright."
But had they marked the stranger's face, and
      seen how all his thought
Was on his own melodious voice—how *self*
      was all he sought—

They would have known that up in Heaven
    that voice was never heard;
That though the *birds* came flying back Christ
    could not hear a word.
The Office ended, lo! they saw beside the Altar
    stand,
With sad and troubled aspect, one of God's
    Angelic band.
" The Lord hath sent me here to know why,
    on this night so blest,
" No Vesper Hymn arose to Heaven, no praise
    to Him addrest?
" Wherefore hath ceased on high to rise the
    offering of your praise,
" Wherefore unheard the melody that ye were
    wont to raise? "
They crossed themselves in holy fear, and bade
    depart the boy
Whom knowing not they had received with
    thankfulness and joy;
Then bursting forth into the chants it was their
    wont to sing,
High up to Heaven their hymn of praise with
    fervent hearts they fling,
And the Angel bare it on with him to Heaven's
    Lord and King.

BROTHER JEROME'S STORY

OBEDIENCE

'TWAS an old Cistercian Convent,
   And its Rule was hard to bear;
It made Heaven a longed-for haven,
   It made this world dark and drear.

And the Abbot so ascetic
   Had no love for aught of earth;
He rejoiced in Fast and Penance,
   And he hated smiles and mirth.

As men loved their brides, so loved he
   The austere Cistercian code,
For each rule would lay his life down,
   For each rule would shed his blood.

Brother Ambrose, the Seraphic,
   Brother Ambrose, full of love
To mankind and to his Brethren,
   Most of all to GOD above,—

Ofttimes in his holy musings
   On the things prepared on high,
For the souls that wait for JESUS
   In their exile patiently,—

Would forget some rule, so trifling
   Scarce it seemed a rule at all,
And then meekly bear his penance,
   Bear it well before them all.

And one day at the refection,
   Being much absorbed in thought,
He had left upon the table
   Some small crumbs, and knew it not.

Knew it not, till Grace was ended,
   When he rose among the rest,
And he sorrowed, not for penance,
   But for holy rule transgressed.

Strictly was it known and written,
  "None may leave or waste his bread";
Strictly was it known and written,
  "None may eat when Grace is said."

To his hand the tiny fragments
  Gathering with exactest care,
He approached the holy Abbot,
  Knelt before him in his chair.

"Father, I have sinned,"—so spake he ;
  "Lost in thought all carelessly,
"Grace was over ere I noted
  "I had still some crumbs by me.

"There I must not leave them lying,
  "And to eat them may not dare.
"What must I then do, my Father,
  "What the penance I must bear?"

Coldly, sternly, then the Abbot :
  "It is well, my son, you know,
"That e'en rules which seem most trifling
  "Holy Monk may ne'er forego.

"Nought is small which is eternal;
   "Shew me now the crumbs from whence
"You have learnt the holy lesson
   "Of *exact* Obedience."

Oped his hand then Brother Ambrose,
   But it held not now the bread—
Pearls of wondrous size and radiance
   Softly gleamed there in its stead.

And he joyed that CHRIST his Master
   Thus his meek Obedience crowned,
That in stern humiliation
   He such mark of grace had found.

BROTHER LAWRENCE'S STORY

THE LOVE OF CHRIST

THE sun shone on her house by day,
  By night the moonbeams fair,
And as of old in Israel
  'Twas never darkness there.
And all the people marvelled much
  To see the wondrous sight;
"She sure must be a saint," they said,
  "Who has unfading light."

"Nay, nay!" spake one, "no saint is she,
  "For she is always gay;
"Her laugh is clear, and bright the smile
  "That on her lips doth play;
"And light and gamesome is her step,
  "For unto her seems life
"More like a child's long game of play
  "Than a Christian's weary strife.

"None ever saw her smite her breast,
"Or ever weep for sin;
"She gathers of the joys of earth,—
"No saint is she, I ween.
"The saints love hardness, vigil, fast,
"And discipline and prayer,
"And what their Master bare for them
"For His dear sake to bear."

Yet still the golden sun by day,
And the pure fair moon by night,
Though darkness might be all around,
With her made always light.
And still the people marvelled much,
The wonder grew apace,
What GOD saw in that lady's soul
To call for such a grace.

The holy Bishop came to her,
And solemnly he spake:
"My daughter, tell me of your fasts,
"And of the food you take."
The lady smiled as to herself,
And answered low and sweet:
"Of divers meats and delicate,
"My lord, I always eat."

"Then plainly answer me, my child,
  "And tell me if you wear
"Beneath that soft and glistening silk
  "A painful robe of hair.
"If thus you take into your life
  "The suffering borne for you;
"If thus the Cross of Calvary
  "You always keep in view."

"My Father," clear she spake again,
  "No robe of hair is mine,
"The linen that I ever use
  "Is white, and soft, and fine."
The holy man, perplexèd sore,
  Turned back upon his way,
And still the moon shone on by night,
  And GOD'S bright sun by day.

And as he journeying left the place
  For some three days behind,
Anon, the while he prayed, there came
  A thought into his mind;
And speeding back once more he reached
  That lady's house full soon,
A pure white house ensilvered o'er
  By rays of winter moon.

" My daughter ! " and his voice was low
   And hushed as if in prayer,—
" Lov'st thou not mickle CHRIST our LORD ?
   And straight there fell on her
A dazzling radiance as from Heaven,
   And such a smile of love,
As Angels nearest to the Throne
   May wear, we think, above.

" He is my Lord, my Love, my All,
   " The Sweetness of my life ;
" He is my Strength in weakness, He
   " Strives with me in the strife.
" I am in Him, and He in me,
   " My only Hope and Stay ;
" In Him I take my rest by night,
   " In Him I work by day.

" My heart is fain to break with joy
   " When on His Love I think,
" 'Neath that sweet burden, save from Him,
   " My soul must faint and sink."
She paused, and then he laid his hand
   Upon her gold-crowned head,
And blessed her with a blessing high
   Ere on his way he sped.

BROTHER GREGORY'S STORY

PUNCTUALITY

BROTHER Cyril rose betimes,
  Loudly birds their lauds were singing,
And the lovely harebells ringing
  Musical their Matin chimes.
Early rose he CHRIST to seek,
In his spirit's depths to speak
  Unto Him Who heareth prayer.
Radiant East with light was glowing,
Cyril's heart with love o'erflowing,
  As he knelt before Him there.
And his soul to JESUS turning
With an eager, loving yearning
Prayed as souls but seldom pray,
Prayed to see the Spring of Day;
Prayed that sin and struggle past,
He might gain his home at last,

In the Kingdom of the Free,
Safe from sin's dark surging sea.

Musical the harebells' chime,
Musical the skylarks' prime,
Loving prayer scarce notes the time,
  So the minutes passed away,
As that spirit GOD-ward poured
All its Heaven-given hoard,
All a holy life had stored
  In his soul's pure treasury ;
Now thanksgiving, now imploring,
Now confessing, now adoring,
Touching earth, yet Heaven-ward soaring
  E'en to GOD's own Throne on high.
When, behold, upon his sight
Dawned a Vision passing bright—
GOD-like Child of radiant Face,
Full of beauty and of grace ;
Never child of man could be
Half so pure, so fair as He.

Prostrate now fell Cyril kneeling,
Heaven its glory seemed revealing,

Glory on his spirit falling,
With a joy half-free, half-thralling,
Scarcely breathing, scarcely praying,
Only voicelessly still saying,
"Mercy, JESU," thus he stays,
Seeking words of prayer or praise,
Words wherein to utter meetly
All the rapture that so sweetly
   Flows and circles round his heart;
Seeking words to use, beseeching
Some high grace, some deeper teaching,
   Some fresh ghostly gift or art.

On his lips the words were hanging,
   Words which holy boon preferred,
When, behold, the heavy clanging
   Of the Prime-bell now was heard.

Must he go, his LORD forsaking,
Earthly things for heavenly taking?
Must he leave that Presence bright,
Pass to darkness from the light?

As he hesitated, pondering
In his soul and mutely wondering

What the LORD would have him do,
Whisper on his spirit falling
Said, " The bell to Chapel calling
" Is the Voice of GOD to you."

Then he passed forth from that Presence,
Which now seemed to him the essence
Of all holy joy and pleasance,
   And he sought the Chapel door.
Nasal was the monks' intoning,
Oh ! it seemed most dull and droning,
Less like singing than like groaning—
   Ne'er had seemed so bad before.
Natheless Cyril bent his mind
In the Psalms and Prayers to find
Him Whom he had left behind
   (So he deemed it) in his cell.
And he prayed with heart and might,
And in GOD and Angels' sight,
'Gainst the devil fought his fight,
   Fought it bravely, fought it well.

When the Office now was ended
In his soul such peace was blended
With a joy unknown before,

That in maze of blessed dreaming,
Of His Heavenly Guest scarce deeming,
　To his cell he turned once more.
Oh! the bliss beyond all guessing,
Well-nigh human soul oppressing!
There with Hand outstretched in blessing,
Smile Eternal Love expressing—
　Stood the Visitant Divine.
And He said: "Hadst thou not gone
"When the bell gave forth its tone,
"I had left thee here alone;
"But I stayed to hear thy boon,
"I will grant it thee full soon.
　"What thou askest shall be thine."
Bending lowly on the floor,
Cyril prayed thus: "Nevermore
　"Let my soul be stained with sin.
"For Thine own sole glory, LORD,
"Unto me this boon accord,
　"Keep me pure, without, within."
Spake the CHRIST: "'Tis given, My son.
"Now thy race on earth is run,
"And another life begun."
On that day, (so legends tell,)
From his convent and his cell,
Where he lived and strove so well,

Holy Cyril went to dwell
  In the land where sin shall cease.
Lying meekly on the ground
They his lifeless body found,
For his loving soul was bound
  To the pilgrims' Home of Peace.

BROTHER BERNARD'S STORY

DILIGENCE

Part I

" I WOT 'tis weary labour mine ; thus day
by day to speed

" To Mary's Well for water fresh for all the
Brethren's need.

" What if 'tis pure and sparkling, and if nowhere
else are found

" Such streams of light and crystal bright as in
her spring abound,

" Methinks with me the labour hard some
Brother now should share,

" Or from some spot more near to home the
water I might bear.

" But now my life and strength and time all
uselessly I spend,

" And 'neath the burden of a mule my shoulders
    I must bend.

" When first the Father unto me this graceless
    task consigned

" Few Brethren were there in the House, and
    well I call to mind

" That but one journey, seldom made, might
    well for all suffice,

" And this day 'neath the sun's hot rays I've
    borne my burden thrice.

" I may not speak, and hard it is that he should
    make me still

" Draw water for the others' use, and climb the
    weary hill,

" Nor send some younger novice now to aid
    me, who alone

" All uncomplainingly for weeks my thankless
    work have done.

" I know that in S. Bridget's Well the water is
    not clear,

" But more than good things distant, I prize
    those which lie more near,

" And oh! how joyful should I be if I were bid
    this night

" To toil no more to Mary's Well for water pure
    and bright ;

"And if the Brethren cannot drink what I
    henceforth should bring,
"Why, each must go himself and fetch his own
    draught from the spring."
So pondered Brother Francis, for in murmuring
    mood was he,
And all the labour that he wrought, he wrought
    unwillingly.
His brow was dark, his glance downcast, and
    when his work was done,
On discontented musing bent he wandered forth
    alone.
It was the happy evening hour when, toil and
    study o'er,
All meet for recreative talk, and Brethren gladly
    pour
Into the listening ear of friends each glowing,
    burning thought,
Or tell of quaintly pictured scenes a skilful hand
    hath wrought,
Or tale recite that one, perchance, in ancient
    tome hath found,
While among all true Charity and kindly ways
    abound.
In cheerful talk, albeit restrained, the happy
    hour passed by,

Till smiles were checked, and words were
    hushed, as Compline hour drew nigh.
None noticed Francis' empty seat, none sought
    him where he stood
Still his own woes relating to himself in the
    green wood,
And musing on his bitter lot, till in that little
    space
Pride and rebellion wrote their name upon the
    Brother's face.
And in the Chapel one might note, while clear
    the voices rose
To ask the blessing of the Lord upon their
    night's repose,
In Te speravi, Domine, did never Francis
    say,
For from his Lord his evil thoughts had borne
    his heart away.
He could not sing *Qui habitat* whose soul
    had wandered on
Far from the shadow of that Rock in Whom we
    trust alone.
And when the *Nunc Dimittis* soft and slow
    arose—I ween—
With close-locked lips, and close-locked heart,
    was Brother Francis seen.

Small grace was his as to his cell he turned in
　　sullen mood ;
He looked not where an imaged CHRIST hung
　　patient on the Rood,
He looked not at the holy words writ on the
　　wall with care,
For his soul was bound, and an evil sprite held
　　cruel empire there.

PART II

" METHINKS, my son," the Abbot spake, and
　　gentle was his voice——
" The tidings that I bring to thee should make
　　thy heart rejoice.
" Thy ceaseless toil mine eyes have seen, thy
　　weary, halting gait,
" As early in the morning chill, and when the
　　day grows late,
" Thou bearest water springing fresh from
　　Mary's Fountain clear,
" Nor e'er hast sought to slake our thirst from
　　wells that rise more near.
" Think not I do not joy in all thy zeal and
　　patience strong,

" In Heaven they know (we doubt it not) that
thou hast laboured long.

" The work I now, for thy relief, to other hands
assign ;

" GOD grant he do as thou hast done when the
hard task was thine."

Confused, the Brother knelt apace, but ne'er a
word spake he,

Deep shame was working in his heart as he
bent there silently.

And he took the boon he had longed for so
with a sense of utter dread,

While the holy Abbot laid his hand in blessing
on his head.

With envious glance his eye still sought the
wood, where hidden lay

S. Mary's Fount, whence Brother Paul drew
water day by day.

And rest from toil seemed unto him a sore and
bitter thing,

A penance, lacking penance's grace—no sweet-
ness, but all sting.

And pondering sadly, half in wrath, and half
repentingly,

He had a vision, and he saw an Angel from on
high

Who, hour by hour, with Brother Paul walked
    all the weary day,
And every footstep reckoned up along the sunny
    way,
And seemed to joy when labour grew, yea,
    seemed full glad indeed,
As more and more of water fresh the thirsty
    Brethren need.
"And did they count my steps," he thought,
    "did GOD's bright angels know
"The many times my aching feet have borne
    me to and fro?
"And did they count my steps?" he thought.
    Anon the Brother heard
A voice responding through the air to his un-
    spoken word—

      "Only loving service
        "High in Heaven is stored,
      "Ne'er a grudging labour
        "Bring we to the Lord.

      "We are sent to gather
        "From His children's hands
      "Whatsoe'er they offer,
        "Work, or gold, or lands.

"Sometimes we may bear Him
" But a loving smile,
"Sometimes words, which, soothing,
" Lonely hours beguile.

"Sometimes earnest labour,
" Sometimes steadfast prayer,
"Sometimes patient suffering,
"Sometimes anxious care.

" But a stinted offering
" He can never own,
" Who the Cross elected
" For His earthly Throne.

" And be sure, those footsteps
" Angels never see,
" Which man cares to reckon
" All complainingly.

" Only willing service
" High in Heaven is stored,
" Ne'er a grudging labour
" Bring we to the LORD."

BROTHER AUGUSTINE'S STORY

BROTHERLY LOVE

DWELT together hermits twain,
   Simple men were they,
Part in prayer and part in toil
   Spent they every day.

And they loved each other well,
   Peaceful was their life,
Never knowing discontent,
   Never knowing strife.

Spake one evening Brother Paul
   "Surely you and I
" Are most ignorant of men!"
   "Tell me, Brother, why?"

" All men save ourselves, I know,
 " Quarrel now and then,
" Only we, not knowing how,
 " Still in peace remain."

" Teach me," mild spake Brother John,
 " How to do my part ;
" I will then, if so you wish,
 " Try with all my heart."

" Lo, this brick," said Brother Paul,
 " Here I place in view,
" And you stoutly must maintain
 " It belongs to you.

" I shall say that it is mine,
 " And if both can well
" Do our part, there shall arise
 " Quarrelling in this cell.

" Now we will begin. I say
 " This is mine own brick."
" Nay, I'm sure that it is mine,".
 Cried the other quick.

D

" If 'tis yours," said Brother Paul,
  " Take it if you will."
Smiling then they saw that strife
  Lay beyond their skill,

Saw that they must be content
  Ever to remain,
'Mid the contests of the world,
  Ignorant old men.

THE ABBOT'S STORY

AN old man knocking at a Convent gate,
Footsore and weary, as though many a
    mile
His feet that day had sped.   A few grey locks
Formed a soft nimbus round the shaven
    head ;
Thought on his brow deep-graven lines had cut,
But there was nought of feeble or of weak
In the erect and wellnigh stately form.
His eye was full of fire, and when he shot
A keen and penetrating glance, but few
Could well resist the power that lay therein.
But now that living glance was full of peace.
A strange smile played upon the old thin
    lips,
A restful, simple smile, as if at length

35

Some long-sought joy was his, and the deep
    lines
Relaxed; and over all his face was shed
A happy look as of a happy child.
He knocked; and when at last one ope'd the
    door,
Meekly he said, his hands crossed on his breast,
His look downcast: " I pray that unto me
" These walls may give a shelter till I die.
" I am an old man, but these hands can work,
" And I can pray, my brother, 'mid the rest.
" Let me then in to rest before I die."
Gravely the Brother: " Sure it is not meet
" To bring to GOD the dregs of your old life ;
" To offer Him a dying tree, from whence
" All fruit and power of bearing fruit is gone.
" Not so, my son, young flowers we gather
    here,
" Fresh flowers all bright with dewdrops of the
    morn
" And fragrant with the graces dear to GOD.
" Pure and unsullied must our offerings be,
" And you, all soiled with a long life ill-spent,
" Would ill befit GOD's chosen garden ground.
" Old man, 'twere mocking GOD to give yourself,
" Renouncing pleasure only when, perchance,

" No longer does the world come wooing you;
" Or it may be that strength no longer serves
" To gain a living, and that dread of want
" Hath sent you here to give yourself to
    God."
" My brother "—and the old man knelt to
    him—
" Oh, take me in ; give me the lowest place,
" Give me the humblest offices to fill ;
" Let me but tend the cattle ; let me dwell
" Amid the swine, and minister to *them*,
" But only let me in."   And so it was,
The earnest pleading won that Brother's heart,
And to the Abbot straight he led their guest.

Years passed away, and Brother Placidus
(For so they styled the old man) sought and
    found
Amid the Brethren there the lowest place.
'Twas his to labour through the live-long day
About the Convent grounds. 'Twas his to
    cleanse
The stables where the Convent horses lived ;
He fed the swine and cared for them, and oft
Fared worse than they. For him as food was
    served

What others left ; and he was ever clad
In garments other Brethren had outworn.
And still each day yet more elastic grew
His springing step, and from his brow were gone
All signs of care.   Right well did he befit
The name of Placidus they gave to him.
And at the Holy Offices his face
Was lit with fire unearthly, and he seemed
Rapt in adoring ecstasy and love.
One day, one sultry day, he—'neath the rays
Of summer's sun—was digging by the gate
Where grew the Father Abbot's favourite
    flowers,
Some tall white lilies.   'Twas but yesterday
He had had penance given him because
Some little weeds the Abbot's eye descried
Among the flowers.   Then he had said : " Old
    man,
" Because *your* life has been all full of weeds,
" Their poisonous presence is as nought to
    you ;
" But take good heed that they approach not
    near
" God's own pure lilies."   So the old man now
This summer's day was toiling in the sun,
And smiling to himself so happily

That one might think, but for the bead-like
    drops
(The gardener's curse) which hung upon his
    brow,
He had some charm to shield him from the
    heat.
One came then knocking at the outer gate,
And as the Brother opened it, the thoughts
Of the old man went back unto that day—
Now three years since—when he stood pleading
    there.
Unto himself he smiles, but looks not up—
Nor cares to know who comes. He looks not
    up,
But one is seizing now his sandalled feet,
And kissing them with full and rapturous joy :
" My Father, have I found thee ? " So he
    spake
'Mid tears and smiles. " Oh ! we have sought
    for thee
" With breaking hearts these three years, and
    our prayer
" Seven times each day to Heaven has gone up ·
" ' O JESU, if it be Thy Holy Will,
" Restore to us our Father ! ' " So he knelt
Still at the feet of Brother Placidus.

" Bless me, my Father."   And the old man laid
Upon the bowed head of the stranger monk
His brown hard hand, and smiling sadly said :
" My son, I bless thee, from my very soul.
" Would it had been GOD's Will to leave me
    here
" Until He takes me to Himself in death !
" But His most Holy Will must needs be done,
" And I must e'en away to power again."
Soon through that Convent it was known to all
That Brother Placidus, whom they despised—
Whom they had oft-times taunted that he gave
Only the dregs of sinful life to GOD—
Was one who fled from power, to seek, for
    CHRIST,
The lowest place.   The Abbot of a House
Where eighty Brethren to his lightest word
Gave prompt obedience ; the Father loved
By all his sons, and loving them again,
He yet had fled ; fearing lest honour here
Might gain for him hereafter endless woe.
He wept to leave his place of lowliness,
But he must go, and as he passed away
Along the garden path his hand had kept—
And through the gate where once he humbly
    sued

To gain an entrance—all the Brethren knelt
And prayed him for his blessing ; and he laid
Upon each head his hand, and thanked them all
For all that they had done for his poor soul.
The Abbot fell down at his feet, and wept ;
And so 'mid mingled blessings, tears, and smiles
Did Placidus, the lowly one, depart.

Miscellaneous Poems and Legends

IN MEMORIAM, J. K.

WE weep not when a master soul hath given
    A voice in music to his spirit-life,
And told in living utterance meet for Heaven
    The thrilling story of his joy and strife.

We weep not when the wondrous work is finished,
    When peals and dies away the last Amen,
Only we prize with rapture undiminished
    The echoes of that high, celestial strain.

Now we have heard on earth the last vibration
   Of a sweet melody, by GOD's Own Hand
Played on the harp-strings of His new creation,
   And full of beauty none save GOD had
     planned.

Oh! one hath passed away from earth for
   ever
   Whose voice was as a "very lovely song
Of one that hath a pleasant voice," and never
   That music now shall sweep our souls
     along.

Yet none can weep—still that sweet measure
   soundeth
   Within the Paradise of GOD on high;
In full perfected beauty it resoundeth
   Where sin can never mar its harmony.

Who weepeth when, the sculptor's work com-
   pleted,
   The Saint on which his hand so long hath
     wrought,
With hymns of exultation oft repeated,
   Into some grand Cathedral niche is brought?

Who mourns to think that never hammer ring-
   ing
Shall strike again the form we love so much—
That chisel never more its sharpness bringing
   Shall smiting wound it with a keen cold
   touch ?

Long time we deemed it faultless, ere the
   Master
Saw it was good, beheld each perfect line—
Then bore it far from danger and disaster,
   And placed it in a Church, beside the
   Shrine.

Now a great Saint, whom GOD's Own Hand hath
   moulded,
   Hath passed away from sorrow and alarms,
Hath shed his latest tear, and is enfolded
   All safely in the Everlasting Arms.

The holy hands so often raised in blessing,
   The thoughtful brow, the bright and tender
   smile,
The mouth severe, that told of self-repressing,
   Are all gone from us for a little while.

We weep not, though our very hearts are riven ;
  " He hath done all things well," we strive to
    say :
" Blest be His Holy Name, for He hath given ;
  " Blest be His Name, for He hath taken
    away."

A THANKFUL HEART

METHINKS of all the sins that pierce the
    Heart of CHRIST anew,
And once again in bitterwise bring Calvary to
    view—
That in those Hands and Feet again the nail-
    prints deep impress—
The blackest is the loveless sin of dark un-
    thankfulness.

A grudging soul that counts its sorrows, weigh-
    ing one by one
The pains it bears, the tears it sheds, the work
    that it hath done ;
That thanks its GOD perchance because it has a
    patient mind,
And for its crowning grace desires a spirit well-
    resigned.

Resigned! that CHRIST hath died for thee upon
    the shameful Tree;
Resigned! that still He lives, and pleads in
    Heaven's high court for thee;
Resigned! that He hath willed to thee His
    Nature to impart,
And that for thee undying love burns in His
    Human Heart!

Or it may be thou art *resigned* to think that thou
    hast borne
One little splinter from His Cross, or from His
    Crown one thorn;
Or that (when contumely pursued thy Master
    year by year)
Some word of censure of thyself hath fallen on
    thine ear.

O sin against the Love of CHRIST of all the sins
    that are,
Methinks that this in Heaven must move the
    greatest sorrow far,
Must make the Soul of CHRIST to grieve and
    Angels' eyes grow dim,
At sight of all He does for us and the nought we
    do for Him.

O grudging hearts ! for very shame be thankful,
    if ye may,
That He allows such coward souls to suffer day
    by day,
That He hath left His Cross on earth, nor carried
    it on high, -
That ye in likeness of His Death may learn of
    Him to die.

"O child," He saith, "of My deep Love unto
    Death's grasp I sped,
"No place had I, save the hard Cross, whereon
    to lay My Head;
"This beauteous earth I made so bright and
    plenteous for thy sake
"Yielded Me not one little spot where I some
    rest could take.

"I made the flowers, the fragrant flowers ; but
    only thorns were found
"To twine into the royal Crown which round My
    Brow was bound !
"I made the fruit, the pleasant fruit ; but none
    was found for Me,
"To slake the burning thirst that rose in My
    Death Agony.

"O child, whom I have loved as never mother
    loved her own,
"O child, whom I have pleaded for at Heaven's
    eternal Throne,
"Think not thy soul can brook to lose one pang
    I send to thee,
"Know that thy griefs and sorrows all are
    measured out by Me.

"Each anxious thought, each sleepless night,
    each unrefreshing prayer,
"Each bitter tear thou shedd'st on earth are in
    high Heaven My care ;
"Each great bereavement, shaking the founda-
    tions of thy life,
"Each unsuccess, each calumny, and all thy
    weary strife,—

"I know them all, I send them all, for very love
    for thee ;
"Take them, My child, as from My Hand, but
    take them thankfully ;
"Be thankful for thy joys, but most be thankful
    for thy woe,
"For he, who ne'er felt grief on earth, ne'er joy
    in Heaven can know."

SUNDAY COLLECTS

THE Church's Beads, we tell them year by
    year,
  And seven long days each lingers in our
    grasp;
For seven long days a several jewel clear
  And bright we're called to look upon and
    clasp.

Then we must let it go, but evermore,
  Ere from our hold the treasure may depart,
If we have made the most of all its lore,
  We ponder sadly in our faltering heart.

O precious chain, of marvellous beauty wrought,
  And flung around the changing course of time,
Whose gems were formed in mines of ancient
    thought,
  When yet GOD'S new creation sang its
    Prime;

Chiselled and cut by lapidaries skilled,—
  Leo, Gelasius, Gregory, grand old men,
With children's hearts and spirits GOD had
    filled,
  They gave the beads that hang upon our
    chain ;

They carved and fashioned every varying
    stone,
  And the Church strung them on a golden
    cord.
Fair are the colours blent in that bright zone,
  And soft the radiance that their tints afford.

As crystal pure of GOD'S own Truth some
    tell,
  While some with Love's gold hue are beauti-
    fied.
There amethysts the fate of sin bewail,
  And rubies with CHRIST'S Blood are deeply
    dyed.

LORD, bind around our hearts this rosary :
  Teach us to use aright from day to day
Each gold-bound jewel of antiquity,
  Till the Day break and shadows flee away.

"THE LORD SHOWED HIM A TREE"
(EXODUS XV. 25)

The Disciple.

SHEW me a Tree, my gracious LORD,
 For o'er my troubled soul
The bitter waters of despair
 In whelming torrents roll;
Thou Who of old, by Marah's tide,
The healing Wood didst swift provide,
Oh! hither speed in Love and Power,
And shed Thy Light on this dark hour.

The Divine Master.

There was a Tree in Eden set
 The day that Adam fell,
A Tree whose sweetness mortal words
 May not essay to tell:
Though 'neath its weight thy weakness sink,
To those dark waters' cheerless brink

Bear it, and cast it boldly in—
It hath Divinest Medicine
The Man of Sorrows' Royal Throne—
That Wood all grief, all woe, hath known.
Dost thou despair? Oh! haste to take
The Cross where I in anguish spake,
"Wherefore, My GOD, dost Thou forsake?"

The Disciple.

Seeking as erst a sweet'ning Tree,
    To Thee, O LORD, I haste,
For heavy on my fainting soul
    The hand of grief is prest.
'Mid bitter foes, 'mid friends grown cold,
Alone I stand: oh! now behold,
And deign in Love the Wood to shew
That can to sweetness change such woe.

The Divine Master.

O hard of heart! hast thou not yet
    Found, hidden in My Cross,
Virtue for all that bitterest seems,
    And gain for every loss?

On Calvary from the shameful Tree
The words were spoken, e'en for thee,
For thee, that thou mayest speak and live—
"They know not what they do, forgive!"

The Disciple.

I stand upon the awful brink
    Of Jordan's bitter stream;
Cold flow its waves—O LORD, my LORD,
    Whose Pity did redeem,
Thou Who in every trial hour
Hast succoured me with saving power,
Cast in the Tree, the sweet'ning Tree,
Lest I be borne away from Thee,
And sink and perish utterly!

The Divine Master.

My child, in passing through that stream
    No evil need'st thou fear;
My Rod and Staff, the holy Cross,
    Sheds sweetness even here;
Take to thee then My words as Shield—
"FATHER, to Thee My soul I yield!"
Stoop to the waves, My Cross shall bear thee o'er,
Calmly and safely bear to Canaan's shore.

"GOD DID SEND ME BEFORE YOU"
(GENESIS xlv. 5)

GOD hath sent a Man before thee!
    Faint not, fear not, Christian soul;
One hath run the race thou runnest,
    One for thee hath won the goal.

GOD hath sent a Man before us!
    Whatsoever griefs oppress,
He hath known them in the fullness
    Of extremest bitterness.

GOD hath sent a Man before us,
    Tried and tempted e'en as we,
Who hath fought our every battle,
    Who hath won the victory.

GOD hath sent a Man before us,
  Not along life's bright highway,
'Mid the beauty and the fragrance,
  And the pleasant light of day;

But in lonely paths and rocky,
  Where we only trace the road
By the Drops of Blood which tell us
  Where the Man of Sorrows trode.

Yea! He sent His CHRIST before us,
  Unto pain and agony;
Not from Death's dark hour withheld Him,
  Willing for our sakes to die.

He within the Veil is entered,
  Where He offers still on high,
Priest and Victim, for our cleansing,
  Sacrifice unceasingly!

THOUGHTS FOR S. JAMES' DAY

OH, youth is very pleasant,
  Its flowers they are so bright,
Half-smiling and half-weeping,
  Bestrewed with dew-drops bright;
Its griefs are half a pleasure,
  Its joys to grief are kin,
As, 'mid mild showers of April,
  Fair rainbow hues are seen.

Oh, life is very pleasant,
  When youth begins to see
How much of joy and loving
  Is scattered full and free.
And all the thorns are hidden,
  And the path seems straight and smooth,
For love's arms are around us
  To gladden and to soothe.

And then, and then, when all things
   Are looking bright and fair,
A mother's fond ambition,
   A father's tender care,
And other love is dawning,
   And all with joy is rife—
We recking nought of sorrow,
   Of sacrifice, or strife—

What if upon our musings,
   And dreams of future time,
To which our glad heart beating
   Rings like a merry chime—
What if, as once it sounded,
   On the Galilean sea,
A Voice to us should utter,
   "Leave all and follow Me,"

Leave all the glowing rosebuds
   Your hand is stretched to take,
Leave all the busy schemings
   Your mind delights to make;
Leave mother's soft caresses,
   Leave your home's sheltering rood,
To drink the cup of sorrow,
   To be baptized in blood?

No more may future visions
  Awake your kindling gaze,
Your castles of home-pleasure
  You to the ground must raze;
From touch and tone that thrilled you
  Turn, turn, nor look again,
The Call that now has reached you
  May not be heard in vain.

Oh joy for those who hear it,
  When in the last dread Day,
In making up His jewels,
  The LORD of Life shall say:
"I was fast bound in prison,
  "The prison-house of sin;
"You broke the iron portals
  "And let Truth's daylight in.
"What ye for Mine have suffered
  "I count as done for Me.
"Come, good and faithful servant,
  "Mine own for aye to be."

LEGEND OF S. FRIDESWIDE

WELL I love the ancient story
   Of the saintly Frideswide told,
She who scorned earth's pomp and glory,
   Worlding's love and worlding's gold.

Where the placid Isis waters
   Fertile plain and forest maze,
Frideswide and her chosen daughters
   Lived a life of prayer and praise.

Well she loved the poor and lonely—
   (Lonely exile she had known)—
Living for her Master only,
   All His loved ones were her own.

Sick and poor in squalid dwelling,
   Helpless widow, orphan sad—
These S. Frideswide sought for, telling
   Of the Love that makes us glad.

To her convent home returning,
  From a weary, toilsome day,
As the evening lamps were burning—
  Crouched a leper by the way.

Gaunt he looked, poor child, and savage;
  All the maidens backward drew,
Misery had made such ravage
  On the face that met their view.

Only Frideswide, gentle mother,
  Cast a look of pitying pain;
Look which kindled in the other,
  Half-despairing, hope again.

"Gentle Frideswide, virgin saintly,
  "Think of JESU's Cross and shame,
"Shun me not," he murmured faintly,
  "Kiss me in His Holy Name."

Horror seized on each beholder;
  Only Frideswide without fear—
(Perfect love had made her bolder)—
  To that living corpse drew near.

Softest kiss of tenderest mother
  On the child's pale lips she pressed—
"In the Name of CHRIST, my brother,
  "May He heal and give thee rest."

Leprous scales are falling slowly
  From the wasted form and face;
One pure touch of maiden holy
  Works this miracle of grace.

Then together thanks they render
  To the mighty GOD above,
Who, by loving hearts and tender,
  Leads men to His greater love.

Wouldst thou learn to comfort sorrow—
  Draw sad hearts from sin and shame?
Holy Frideswide's safeguard borrow,
  Love and help in JESU's Name.

EADGITH AND ESICA

AN ANGLO-SAXON LEGEND

IN her lonely cell knelt Eadgith—
  Bitter, bitter tears she wept;
Through the hours when sorrow sleepeth,
  Cold and weary watch she kept—
For her loved and dying nursling
  Sadly prayed while others slept.

Life for her holds nothing dearer
  In this earthly dwelling-place;
Death is coming nearer, nearer,
  Death is coming on apace—
"Spare my Esica," she pleadeth,
  "Spare him but a little space."

Babe forsaken, she had found him
  In the hovel where he lay;

And her heart had twined around him,
  Close and closer day by day,—
Must the angels bear him from her
  To the country far away?

And her tears are falling faster,
  Down her cheeks they pour like rain,
As she prays the Heavenly Master
  That her child she may detain,
But a little, little longer,
  From His holy virgin-train.

Hark! a sound is falling
  On her startled ear,
Like a sweet voice calling—
  (There is no one near)—
And her heart is thrilling
  With a nameless fear.

" Eadgith, Eadgith, Eadgith,"—
  'Tis the well-known voice,
Sweeter far than music,
  Needs must she rejoice.

Like a bell at even,
  Bidding labour cease,
Came that voice from Heaven,
  Telling of release,—
"Toil and pain are over,
  " Enter into peace."

Keenest pain is thrilling through her,
  It is welcome to her heart ;
Death, kind death, that cometh to her,
  Cannot keep the twain apart,
He must needs these loving spirits
  Knit together with his dart.

She is falling, falling, falling,
  (So it seems) through endless space ;
But she hears the sweet voice calling
  From the Heavenly dwelling-place,
Where the ransomed bathe their spirits
  In the light of JESU's Face.

As bewildered child rejoices
  In the forest's trackless gloom,

When he hears the sound of voices
Crying—"This way lies your home,"
So to Eadgith came the signal
That she need no further roam.

Spake the Sisters sadly,
"She too must depart,"
But she heard it gladly,
With a thankful heart.

When the bell for Vespers
Summoned them to prayer,
Softest angel whispers
Charmed the listening air,—
"Where her nursling waiteth
"We her soul shall bear."
Ere the fiery sun-ray
Lighted up the west,
In the brighter country,
Region of the blest,
Esica and Eadgith
Had attained their rest.

"IF THY PRESENCE GO NOT WITH ME, CARRY US NOT UP HENCE"

(Exodus xxxiii. 15)

O EARNEST prayer wrung out of heart
half-broken
At bitter thought of plenty all unblest,
Revealing somewhat of the love unspoken
　　That glowed within a Saint's heroic breast ;

Revealing somewhat of a spirit burning
　　With thirst intenser than the desert's drought,
Of a deep agonising nameless yearning
　　For Peace such as this earth hath never
　　　wrought.

What was to him the pleasant land o'erflowing
　　With milk and honey, and the gladdening vine?
What were the wells of water ever flowing,
　　And what the hidden treasures of the mine?

Nought recked he of a silver river gliding
  'Twixt golden banks of richly waving corn,
Except the presence of his GOD abiding
  Might feed his soul, else desolate, forlorn.

Better, far better, in the desert lonely,
  Still to draw out the measure of his life,
To bear the people's murmurings still, if
    only
  That Presence might be with him in the
    strife;

If only day by day his soul adoring
  Might commune with his Saviour in the
    cloud,
If only night by night his spirit soaring
  Might penetrate the GODHEAD'S radiant
    shroud.

Full of all pain and weariness and sorrow
  Had been the journey from Egyptus' coast;
But oh! the darkness of that sadder morrow
  Which should behold the LORD forsake His
    host.

And we can echo, with unfaltering voices,
  The prayer which GOD'S great hero prayed
    of yore :
In JESU'S Love the faithful heart rejoices ;
  If He be with us, what hath Heaven of more?

The gold-paved street and each fair pearly
    portal,
  The crown, the palm, the robe of glistening
    white, ·
The songs of Angels, and long life immortal,
  Without Him would be dark and desolate
    night.

"LORD, if Thy Presence go not with us wholly,
  "Carry us not up hence," but evermore,
Kneeling on earth before some Altar lowly,
  Let our hearts only love Thee and adore.

SONG FOR CHILDREN

DO you ask, O child of Jesus,
   What the Lord will have from you?
Are you pondering in your spirit
   What your little hands may do?
O dear child, so loved in Heaven,
   Signed with Christ's own saving Sign,
I will tell how in His treasury
   He stores gifts as small as thine.

I will tell you how a lily,
   Pure and white and very fair,
When the Lord for us was bleeding
   Poised her snowy chalice there,
Fearing lest those Drops so sacred
   On the soilèd earth should lie,
All neglected, all uncared for,
   And forgotten utterly.

And the LORD, to crown the worship
  Of the lovely lily flower,
Bids her wear the spots of crimson
  As a glory to this hour.
And we love the spotted arum,
  For it tells how CHRIST will prize
Lowly deeds of loving service
  And will own them in the skies.

I will tell you, little children,
  How a bird with breast now red,
While the lilies mutely worshipped,
  Hovered round the Saviour's Head.
Men were jeering, men were scoffing,
  But that loving bird would fain,
If perchance it might do something,
  On the Cross with CHRIST remain.

And it marked the crown of anguish,
  And with pain drew forth one thorn
From that diadem of suffering,
  Pressed upon those Brows in scorn.
And the LORD, to own the service,
  Marked its breast with roseate hue:
Christian children, bought by JESUS,
  Is there nought that you can do?

Pure as lilies, and as buoyant
   As the birds that cleave the skies,
Seek and strive with earnest longing,
   Seek for things to sacrifice.
Little pence and little moments,
   Lay them down before the LORD;
Though He give no outward token,
   In His Heart your gifts are stored,
And a Day is surely coming
   When your offering He will own:
Hasten, Christian children, hasten,
   Cast your gifts before His Throne.

VANDREGISIL

IN the hoary days of eld,
  In the palace royal,
Dagobert a revel held
  With his barons loyal.

Vandregisil rode perplexed
  To his monarch's dwelling;
Many thoughts his spirit vexed,
  In his bosom swelling.

From his youth he had obeyed
  One of Kingdom vaster,
From his boyhood he had made
  CHRIST his feudal Master.

And the service of *that* Court
  Was to him far dearer
Than the boisterous noise and sport
  Every hour brought nearer.

But the king, who loved him well,
  Gave him no releasing,
Called him from his quiet cell
  For the Christmas feasting.

" Ho! what means this noisy shout
  " By the king's own dwelling?
" And what means this rabble rout,
  " Every moment swelling? "

" Here is nought to move thine ire;
  " But a clumsy peasant
" Struggling vainly in the mire—
  " Ah! the jest is pleasant."

" Lift thy waggon, heavy hand—
  " Floundering hither, thither!
" Would'st thou swim upon the land
  " As in yonder river? "

None will take the peasant's part;
  On his form they trample!
Strangers to the loving Heart
  Of our Great Example.

Swiftly Vandregisil sprung
From his charger fiery,
Little recked of taunting tongue,
Cart-tracks deep and miry.

On his feet the peasant stands,
Now his cart is righted;
May he kiss those noble hands
All too ill requited?

"Mud upon his tunic rich,
"All his courtly raiment;
"Lifting beggars from the ditch,
"'Tis his proper payment."

Loud the taunting laughter rang,
Wherefore should he fear it?
'Twas as if a small bird sang,
Scarcely did he hear it.

"What will be thy guerdon now
"In the royal presence?
"Scornful look and frowning brow,
"Patron saint of peasants!"

Onward Vandregisil strode,
   Grand he looked and stately;
He who greatly fears his GOD
   Fears **not** others greatly.

Now in presence of the king
   He his head is baring;
Whispered words go round the ring
   Of his pride and daring.

Solemn pause the monarch made,
   Looked upon him coldly,—
"Wherefore, sir, in masquerade,
   "Comest thou thus boldly?"

"Good my liege, my brother lay
   "At thy gate despairing;
"Could I on this joyful day
   "Pass him by uncaring?

"GOD the poor man honoureth,
   "Taking his condition;
"One Poor Man of Nazareth
   "Saved **us** from perdition."

Such a smile the king's face wore
  Not before or after;
All who stood beside the door
  Ceased their scornful laughter.

"Look," said he, "and fix your gaze
  "On this soilèd raiment;
"So the world its heroes pays
  "With a sorry payment.

"But to me these mud-stains are
  "Jewels fair and royal,
"Sent by One Who dwells afar
  "To His servant loyal.

"From the vanguard of His host
  "I have long detained thee;
"I, because I loved thee most,
  "All these years restrained thee.

"Now I yield thee up to One
  "Of a Kingdom vaster,—
"To the FATHER'S Royal SON,
  "CHRIST, thy feudal Master."

ABBOT STEPHEN

TO Abbot Stephen the cellarer spake—
  "Sad news, my Father, our silence
    break,
  " And sadder are yet in store;
" There is no food left in the house to-day,
" The last of our helpers has passed away,
" No bread can I on the table lay,
  " And we fast till we can no more.'

But bright was the look in the Abbot's eyes,
And he heard the news with a glad surprise,
  Which filled them with happy dew;
For many a year he had followed the road
Which was tracked with the Blood of a suffer-
    ing GOD,
And to set his feet where the Master trod
  Was joy to the servant true.

" Are we like the fowls of the air ? " said he,
" With no food stored in our granary,
      " With nought but our FATHER'S care ?
" Let us go and seek for the crumbs that fall
" From the Table of Him Who feeds us all—
" In the field, in the wood, in the cottage and
      hall,
      " Let us go in the might of prayer."

Then he called to his side a Brother true,
Meet for the work which he had to do,
      And said, " Let us go and glean ;
" To-day at least we are verily poor,
" We will beg for our bread from door to
      door,
" We will bear with joy what our Master bore
      " For love of us sinful men."

Long time they toiled in the summer heat,
(To suffer with JESUS to them was sweet
      As rest to the weary head,)
And they met at eve when the shadows fell,
Within the sound of the vesper-bell,
By the side of an ancient moss-grown well,
      To reckon how each had sped.

"In truth, my son," said the Abbot blithe,
'Thou hast mown to-day with a stronger
    scythe,
  "Thy burden is more than mine."
And the Brother showed, with a guileless mirth,
Good store of the good things of the earth,
For of fine white bread there was no dearth,
    Nor of wholesome herbs and wine.

"The Priest who dwells where the mill you
    see
"With a great good will gave this to me;"
    But the Abbot's face grew sad.
"To touch it, my son, were a deadly sin;
"Like a wolf to the fold he entered in,
"By an evil bribe his place did win,
    "The gift that 'makes wise men mad.'"

Full sad was the Brother now, I wot,—
But the Abbot Stephen he heeded not,
    Light flashed in his keen blue eye.
"May the GOD of Heaven forbid it me,
"That the wages of this iniquity
"Should serve as food to our monastery,
    "Though we monks should faint and
    die!"

Some simple shepherds stood round about,
The strangers' voices had called them out
 From the fields where their sheep they fed.
The Abbot noticed their wistful look,
From the wallet the herbs and wine he took,
And into their laps the last crumb shook
 Of the Priest's polluted bread.

Then back to their Convent home they went
To a meal as scanty as meal in Lent,
 And they rendered thanks to GOD—
Who fed them as He Elijah fed
With the cruse of water and blackened bread,
That they in the desert might learn to tread,
 As His way to Heaven He trod.

THE NUNS OF BEVERLEY

A CHRISTMAS LEGEND

THE last of the midnight Mass was said
 In the Convent Chapel fair ;
And as to their quiet cells they passed,
A wondering look the Sisters cast
 On the two still kneeling there.

The fast had been strict, the watch was cold,
 And their frames were slight and young,
And their faces wore the snow-drift hue,
But Heaven shone out from their eyes of blue
 As they joined the Angels' song.

They rose at last with a quiet sigh,
 As they sought the corridor—
"Sister," said one, "ere we take our rest,
"On this dear night, of all nights the best,
 "Let us kneel for one prayer more."

82

The sun stole out from a bank of clouds,
 And the Sisters still knelt on ;
Little recked they of time or space,
Whom the Angels had borne to the brighter
  place,
 Where the happy dead are gone.

Oh ! words cannot paint the peace divine
 Of that refuge from the storm ;
When like pictured panes in sunset glow,
The light of Heaven was shining through
 Each noble shadowy form.

But still from the thronging band of Saints,
 Their eyes would onward rove ;
For Heaven itself were a dreary place,
Without one glorious Form and Face,
 To the heart that has learnt to love.

He came—for they saw the wounded Feet,
 The wounds that they knew so well—
No word of love could the Sisters say,
But low at those dazzling Feet they lay
 In a bliss unspeakable.

A moment of bliss it seemed to them !
　　But down on the earth below,
Hour after hour was speeding by,
Till the stars looked forth from the evening
　　sky
　　On the earth in her veil of snow.

Then the Abbess spoke to a faithful nun,
　　Who was waiting at her side :
"These children," she said, "are absent long ;
'The fast has been strict, their frames are
　　young ;
　　"Go see thou if aught betide."

'Rise, Sisters, rise, for the Abbess waits,
　　"You are slow indeed to rise "—
As the voice broke through their blissful trance,
They said with a saddened countenance,
　　"We have been in Paradise."

Oh ! strange it seemed from that world of bliss
　　To turn to this world of woe ;
But a soft voice whispered "This very day "—
They rose together, and took their way
　　To the Convent choir below.

Pardon and blessing they knelt to gain
    From their Mother that Christmas night;
So dazzling the light on each fair young face,
That scarce could the Abbess skill to place
    Her hand on their heads aright.

Low, low they bent on the Chapel floor—
    "Rise, children," the Abbess said—
No voice or motion disturbed the air,
The spirits of those who were kneeling there
    Had returned to the happy dead.

ABSOLUTION

WHEN Jesus by His Word of Power
    Called Lazarus from his loathsome grave,
In type He showed to thoughtful minds
    How He the soul from sin would save.

He spake the word, forthwith the dead
    Awoke and heard its LORD's behest;
But motionless it still remained,
    'The limbs with grave-clothes tightly pressed.

Again the LORD of Glory spake,
    "Loose him and let him go," He said;
And now behold the work complete,
    He lives and moves who late was dead.

Thus still CHRIST smites the sin-bound heart,
    And bids repentant tears to flow.
But to His Priests He gives command,
    "Loose ye him now and let him go."

THE PROMISE TO THE PENITENT

SORROWING one, who weepest sore,
Lo! thy past I will restore.
All the years consumed and lost
By the locusts' swarming host—
(By the restless joys of earth,
Noisy, Heaven-forgetting mirth),
By the cankerworm of care,
And the anguish of despair;
I will give them back to thee,
See thou use them all for **Me**.
Thou hast known the "former rain,"
Storms of sorrow, tears of pain;
Now My "latter rain" shall come,
Making the waste places bloom—
Now the "Corn, and Oil, and Wine,"
Food from Heaven, shall all be thine.
Now My Spirit I will pour
On thy soul redeemed of yore;

No more shame, nor grief, nor tears,
No more self-approaching fears—
Pardoning words thy day shall brighten,
Dreams of Heaven thy darkness lighten.
All is thine—the past is gone ;
Rise up, O thou sorrowing one.

EQUALITY

" So much there is of the more, so much there is of the less."

Old Proverb.

O DEEPEST truth, in homeliest language
 vested,
 And borne down to us from the days of old ;
How many hearts have paused awhile and
 rested
 Upon the wisdom that thy words enfold !
GOD's ways are equal : he whose present store
Hath much of less, hath also much of more.

So much the more of smiles and soft caressing,
 Of exultation in earth's wealth of love :
So much the less of the CHRIST-spoken blessing,
 That those who weep shall heavenly comfort
  prove ;
So much the less GOD's Hand shall be brought
 nigh,
No need to wipe the tear from tearless eye.

So much the more the little stars are shining,
   So much the less of Heaven's glorious sun ;
So much the longer 'mid fair flowers reclining,
   So much the less of toilsome journey won :
God's law of compensation round us lies,
And weighs the earth with balance from the
     skies.

The fragrant flowers that round thy cross are
     wreathing
   Lessen thy part in Jesu's Crown of Thorn :
The praise of thee that friends are fondly
     breathing,
   Oh ! flee ; seek rather for contempt and
     scorn :
Each breath of human praise thou hearest now
Dims the bright crown preparing for thy brow.

So much the more of bitter sin-confessing,
   So much the less of shame in that dread
     Day;
So much the more of heavenly wealth possessing,
   So much the less of goods that pass away :
Ye cannot serve two masters, evermore
Choose then the less in choosing still the
     more.

S. NICHOLAS TO S. R.

YOU have entered on a journey, child, and
none, save GOD, can know
How rough, or long, or dangerous is the way
you have to go;
But this you know, that CHRIST Himself is ever
at your side,
All through the day, until you reach the goal at
eventide.
Then turn not to the left hand, child, and turn
not to the right;
But set your face full steadfastly to walk in
JESU's might:
And hasting not, and resting not, with a strong
heart of love,
And with a rock-like trust in GOD, which nothing
can remove,
Fight, toil, pray—the end will come, the end of
grief and strife,

When sin and death **and** sorrow shall be
    swallowed up of life.
Haste not, **my** child ; rest **not**, my child : but
    toil and pray and fight,
Till the Gates of **New** Jerusalem your longing
    gaze delight,
And He Whom, unseen, you have loved, shall
    be revealed to sight.

Mission
Poems and Ballads

CHRISTMAS

CAN angels weep?—for surely if they can,
    Each Christmas night their tears must
    freely flow,
In thinking of GOD's endless love to man,
    And that first Christmas night long years
    ago.

In thinking how the Bridegroom from above
    From forth the courts of heavenly glory
    sped—
Rejoicing sped—to run his race of love,
    From Bethlehem's manger to His last hard
    bed.

In thinking how exultant then they sang
  Their new-learnt Antiphon of heavenly mirth,
While through the skies the echo sweetly rang,
  "Glory to GOD, and peace upon GOD's earth."

And how the earth, to greet her Maker, found
  And straightway donned her robe of purest
    hue ;
And with bright stars for jewels, richly crowned,
  Stood, queen-like, 'neath her canopy of
    blue—

Knowing the Heavenly Gardener now was come
  To plant again the Tree of Life below ;
To take away her ancient curse and doom,
  To bid fair Eden's flowers once more to blow.

And they remember how their souls went forth
  In floods of rapturous joy, to think that now
Full soon upon the earth, from south to north,
  From east to west, all hearts to GOD would
    bow.

Full soon they thought—alas ! how many a time
  Have they since watched the Christmas feast
    come round,

And sadly listened to the Christmas chime,
   And mourned to note how few the CHRIST
   have found.

How have they longed with burning zeal that
   they
   Might burst the barriers GOD has sent to
   them—
Might speak as on the first great Christmas Day,
   And far and wide glad tidings loud proclaim;

Might show the myriads who in darkness dwell
   That in the east the Day-spring has arisen,
And to men fettered by their sins might tell
   That One is come to visit them in prison.

But no, these heavenly watchers must be dumb,
   Wait with crossed hands, in grieved and sad
   surprise;
They can but pray that soon the hour will come,
   When man to Heaven may lift his heavy eyes.

And *we?*—We joy our Christmas feast to keep
   We twine our garlands, prizing every flower;
While souls are perishing a thousand deep,
   Passing away with every passing hour;

While watchful hosts of sorrowing angels stand
   And mutely mourn, and mutely wonder
     more—
Watching the vessels drifting from the land,
   Watching the thoughtless dwellers on the
     shore.

LORD, give us zeal to work for Thee betimes,
   Early and late to toil unwearying ;
That so the sound of Thy glad Christmas chimes
   Unto our souls no sad reproach may bring ;

That so we, kneeling at Thine altar throne,
   May there with pure and loving heart adore ;
That so in the last day Thou may'st us own
   As Thine—yea, LORD, as Thine for ever-
     more.

THE MOUNT OF OLIVES

THE soul hath holy memories without
    measure,
In thinking of the ancient hills of GOD,
And most it jealously delights to treasure
    Dreams of the sacred spots where CHRIST
    hath trod.

Awe comes with Sinai: softer memories hover
    Around the Mount of sweet Beatitude;
While love, like a fair cloud, hangs always over
    The Calvary where was reared the Holy
    Rood.

But on the brow of Olivet for ever
    Lingers a glory, bright beyond compare—
A Trinity of blessing such as never
    Our thoughts can fathom while we ponder
    there.

H

It speaks of Jesus in a threefold seeming,
  Of Him that was, and is, and is to come;
It gathers up in one His work redeeming,
  And speaks in certain tone of future doom;

Of Him that Was—was in our human fashion;
  Of midnight prayers in the chill midnight air;
Of love divine—immeasurable compassion—
  In agonised petitions poured out there;

Of human suffering, and of human shrinking
  From mental agony none else could know;
Of all the terrible anguish and heart-sinking
  Which perfect knowledge must on man
    bestow.

It tells all this. We can but pray in gazing
  Where the God Man was instant in strong
    prayer,
And prostrate fall—to Him our spirit raising,
  Who for our sake so oft knelt prostrate there.

Of Him that Is—the spot which saw His
    pleading,
  When drops of blood fell from Him on the
    ground,

Tells us that now, in Heaven interceding,
  He, GOD and Man, upon His Throne is
    found.

He loved thee, Olivet, and as 'twas given
  To thee to be His place of strife below,
He chose thee, when returning back to Heaven,
  As the last scene on earth His steps to
    know.

He names thee as the hill where He, returning
  To be our Judge, will plant His piercèd Feet;
When, sheep from goats and wheat from tares
    discerning,
  He to each soul its recompense will mete.

Will He find faith — the Long-suffering, the
    Tender—
  'Mid ransomed souls He wrestled so to
    gain?
Alas! the reckoning man will sadly render
  Of talents wasted—lent, but lent in vain.

Will He find faith? We sleep while souls are
    dying—
  The souls for which He strove on Olivet;

We mourn earth's sin, perchance, and spend, in
    sighing,
    Time which might win to CHRIST some wan-
      derer yet.

We sit with folded hands while nations perish;
    Oh for a voice glad tidings to proclaim
To those whom CHRIST hath left for us to
    cherish,
    Who ne'er have heard the blessèd Saviour's
      name!

Speak, Olivet, to pulseless spirits warning;
    Bid us expect the coming of the LORD;
Bid us toil on till Heaven's own daylight
    dawning
    Brings rest from toil—to labour rich reward.

THE CONVERSION OF POMERANIA

TO-DAY is Stettin full of joy,
    And gladsome is the throng
That through the street bedecked with
    flowers
    Moves merrily along.

It is a feast-day of their god,
    And precious gifts they bear,
With dance, and song, and joyous mien,
    Unto his temple there.

For this have rarest flowers been reared,
    For this bright gems been heaped;
For this is wove the texture fine—
    The golden corn is reaped.

Nature's best gifts, art's choicest works,
    They bring together now—
These generous souls, who as one man
    Before an idol bow.

Among the crowd an old man stands,
    Full weary seemeth he,
Weary of travel—wearying more
    That saddest sight to see—
Men, earnest men, at a false shrine
    Bow down the willing knee.

Strange, 'mid that concourse gay to mark
    This man so full of thought;
His eye gleamed bright, as in his soul
    A mighty fire there wrought:
The fire of Heaven-enkindled love,
    These erring souls which sought.

Long had he cherished hope that GOD
    Would give him grace to win
Unto Himself the Stettin men
    From heathendom and sin.

"Guide me, O LORD : unmeet am I
　"Thy glory to proclaim ;
"Give me a mouth and wisdom now
　"To preach Thy Holy Name."

Wondering, they marked the stranger there,
　But gave him welcome free ;
And bade him eat and drink, and join
　In their bright revelry.

"Not *yours*," most earnestly he cried,
　"But *you*, my sons, I seek !"
And then, with eager, fervent words,
　Of CHRIST he straight did speak :
Of all His lowliness, of all
　His suffering and His love ;
He told of death and judgement hour,
　And of the life above.

Keen was his glance : his words flowed on
　In strong impassioned course ;
You would have thought no human heart
　Could well resist their force.

They listened while he spoke, though some
    With fierce and angry look,
As if the insult to their gods
    Their spirit ill could brook.

And when the torrent of his words
    Ceased for a little while,
One answered him, in gentle tone,
    With half-contemptuous smile:

"Old man, the GOD whom you adore
    "Is not the GOD for us:
"Perhaps He suits the poor, but we
    "Could never worship thus.

"The gods we own are rich and strong,
    "Nor pain nor death may know;
"We love to bring them costliest gifts,
    "Their splendour forth to show.

"Freely they give, and freely we
    "Pour out before their shrines
"The produce of their own fair fields,
    "The treasures of their mines.

"All that we have and all we are
　"Our hearts with joy would yield,
"The glorious altars of our gods
　"From impious hands to shield.

"Go back, old man; to others preach;
　"Unwise your CHRIST must be
"Who sends, to win men unto Him,
　"Ambassadors like thee.

"Go back, old man, ere ill befall,
　"To linger here is vain;
"Preach to the mean of a mean GOD,
　"But not to Stettin men."

They thrust him from the city gate;
　Their jeers fell fast as rain;
He wept the while that not to him
　'Twas given these souls to gain.

A year has passed.　The self-same crowd
　Meet in the gay-decked streets,
While echo in a thousand tones
　The sounds of joy repeats.

On to the temple—on they pass,
  With flowers and garlands gay,
While each and all, with dance and song,
  Their gladsome homage pay.

When suddenly each voice is hushed,
  All breathless, awe-struck stand,
As through the open city gate
  There comes a mighty band.

A mighty band, for surely GOD
  Is in their midst this day—
The day that Otto comes to win
  The land from heathen sway.

He comes not poor: he deems not well
  To come in humble guise;
With dove-like simpleness he blends
  The lore of serpent wise.

With pomp, and state, and regal mien,
  He (lowliest 'mid the low)
Is well content these souls to seek,
  If CHRIST they thus may know.

And first a white-robed band advance,
    Who sing, in joyous wise,
An ancient chant, whose cadences
    Rise to the very skies.

A tone of grave triumphant joy,
    It thrills each heart within;
And whispers of things high and low,
    GOD's glory and man's sin:

"Let GOD arise, and let His foes
    "Be scattered in His sight!
"Let all that hate the Holy One
    "Flee swift before His might!

"As dew in face of burning sun,
    "As wax before the flame,
"Let the ungodly perish now
    "At GOD's most Holy Name."

A symbol rich they bear aloft—
    It glitters in the light—
Of gold and purest silver wrought,
    And lustrous jewels bright.

With many-tinted hues it glows,
  As it is borne along,
While riseth still melodiously
  To Heaven the thrilling song.

And in the midst, with stately step,
  Is mitred Otto seen,
Arrayed (as GOD'S own priest befits)
  In robes of glittering sheen.

Calmly the fair procession comes:
  All stand amazed to see,
So suddenly, within their midst,
  This goodly company.

Of glorious King, of glorious realm,
  Did Otto straightway speak;
How he was sent ambassador,
  These subject-souls to seek;

Of One, man's Maker and his GOD,
  All powerful and all great,
Who (since with man was His delight)
  Had laid aside His state;

As Man had lived, as Man had died,
  This King, the GOD eterne;
Had risen from the dead, and then
  Did to His Throne return;

Of all His state, His might, His power,
  Of all His wondrous love,
And of the gifts divine He showers
  From treasuries above;

And how He holds His court on earth,
  The homage to receive
Of noble souls, whose keen-eyed faith,
  Not seeing, can believe.

"And ye—when all the world is bright
  "With rays from JESUS' Throne—
"Ye still, in darkness and in death,
  "A lying worship own.

"But we have grieved and wept for you,
  "And GOD hath sent us now
"To cast down every idol shrine
  "Where ye so blindly bow."

"Nay, Triglav will avenge his own!"
　Wrathful, cried Triglav's priest,
As round the people stood amazed,
　When Otto's voice had ceased.

"We fear them not. We go to smite
　"Your gods of wood and clay;
"If they be gods, then let them now
　"Their power divine display."

From temple unto temple then
　The long procession passed,
And everywhere each idol form
　Down to the ground they cast.

They entered into secret shrines,
　Where only priests might stand,
With axe and hammer laying low
　The altars of the land.

"Behold the gods in whom ye trust!"
　Cried Otto, full of scorn;
"Behold their fragments, as they lie,
　"From forth their niches torn.

"Oh, wherefore do they not arise,
"And smite us all this day?
"Oh, wherefore do these mighty gods
"Our arm of flesh obey?"

Amazed, the crowd, this festal day,
Whose sun had risen so bright,
Beheld the gods in whom they hoped
Lie prostrate in their sight.

"Call ye on them as here they lie,
"In helpless ruin thrown;
"Nay, while, my sons, 'tis called to-day,
"Kneel, the true GOD to own—

"The GOD Who nerved our hands to break
"These impious forms of stone;
"The GOD Who made you, and Who longs
"To have you for His own.

"Only kneel down and humbly say,
"'CHRIST, teach us to believe!'
"And He that faltering prayer of yours
"With favour will receive."

Now Triglav's priest had slunk away;
   And as one man the crowd,
With fervent prayer for faith and life,
   Before the Saviour bowed.

O happy day, when o'er their brows,
   To seal them for the LORD,
To cleanse them from the stains of sin,
   The healing flood was poured!

But dark and sad their history's page
   When once again they yearned
For evil gods and evil rites,
   And far from JESUS turned!

Till their Apostle, full of love,
   Great Otto, came once more,
And, wakening tears of grief and shame,
   Those souls from error tore.

To few on earth 'tis given to do
   Such work as Otto did;
And most time from the eyes of men
   Their labour's fruit is hid.

Then praise we Him Who gave His Saint
  That mark of favour dear,
To sow the seed, to mark the growth
  Advancing year by year,
From seed to blade, until there rose
  " The full corn in the ear."

But be our prayer as David's was,
  Who only might begin
Great work for GOD, because his hands
  Were stained with blood and sin.

" LORD, show Thy servants of Thy work,
  " And let their children see
" Thy glory, and some fruit of all
  " We fain would do for Thee,
" That Thou be glorified both now
  " And through eternity."

SOLOMON'S KINGDOM

IT fills our mind, that marvellous Bible-
   story—
  Like some wild fabulous tale of Eastern lore;
Where GOD-like wisdom, boundless wealth and
   glory,
  Flow freely from an all-imagined store.

We almost seem to see the gold, the spices,
  The gorgeous peacocks, and the ivory—
The precious gems, and all that still entices
  The eager fancy and the wandering eye.

We almost seem to see the homage duteous,
  The deep obeisance, and the offerings rare,
The glittering tissues, and the carvings beau-
   teous;
  Almost we breath the richly perfumed air.

And as there stands before our wondering vision
  That strange, bright picture of great David's
    Son,
We marvel, if to waken earth's ambition
  The Spirit wrote the tale of Solomon.

Was it to bid us treasure upon treasure,
  And gold uncounted, here to heap below?
Was it to bid us joy by wealth to measure,
  And earthly glory as our bliss to know?

Not so. The Spirit in this tale discloses
  A deep Apocalypse of things on high;—
The gates of Heaven in parable uncloses;
  Eternal joys in symbol bringeth nigh.

One figure only fills the sacred story,·
  And makes the fullness of the Spirit's strain—
Sometimes in suffering, sometimes wrapt in
    glory,
  He, Whose delight is with the sons of men.

The kingly David he who sang and sorrowed—
  As never since hath sung and sorrowed man—
All the deep lustre of his story borrowed
  From Him, Whose Cross therein we dimly
    scan.

And in great Solomon's unnumbered treasures,
    And in the wonders of his golden reign,
Some glimpse of Heaven's joy and endless
    pleasures,
    And of CHRIST's glorious kingdom, we may
    gain.

Kings from the East, their kingly offerings
    laying
Before that Monarch, wise and large of heart,
Are "kings and priests" of CHRIST, who, toiling,
    praying,
    Bring wandering souls in Him to have their
    part.

See Sheba's queen, for highest wisdom yearning,
    Come from afar Jerusalem's King to greet—
See her, with generous hand, ere home return-
    ing,
    Her royal presents fling beneath his feet.

Our Glorious King is building the foundations
    Of His own New Jerusalem on high ;
But lo! He waits for tribute from the nations—
    The living stones, He loves, to be brought
    nigh.

"*Pray* for Jerusalem's peace," for peace is
    lacking
  Until we bring the stones to build the shrine ;
Work for Jerusalem's peace, with might attack-
    ing
  (For it may yield Him gems) each guarded
    mine.

Dig on, through crust of sin and crust of error ;
  Dig on, for royal gems and gold lie deep !
Untiring strive, and be your only terror
  Lest you no gifts before your King may heap.

SPOILING THE EGYPTIANS

HE brought them forth with silver fair, with
    silver and with gold,
Forth from the land of bondage, forth from the
    oppressor bold :
What tho' the toil had been so sore ; what tho'
    severe the fight ;
Yet not "one feeble person" was within their
    tents that night.

They passed away in stately wise from dark
    Egyptus' coast,—
Right glad the foe to see them go ; they feared
    Jehovah's Host,—
And as they pressed to Peace and Rest from
    tyranny untold,
He brought them forth with silver, yea, with
    silver and with gold.

O ye who haste to shelter blest from this world's
    glare and heat,
As on ye pass to Paradise with worn and bleed-
    ing feet,
Spoil well the foe, before ye go,—ye shall not
    meet him there,
For, since the first great Easter Eve, that gate
    he may not dare.

Yea, spoil the foe, before ye go ; from every keen
    device,
From every sore temptation, glean your hoards
    for Paradise ;
From fervent love, the brightest gold your eager
    souls shall win,
And silver, seven times purified, from conquest
    over sin.

Yea, spoil the foe, before ye go ; and while ye
    keep with care
The flower that blows, the fruit that glows, in
    your own vineyard fair,
Bear home to CHRIST, as gifts unpriced, those
    whom He died to gain ;
For thy one soul redeemed by Him, see that
    thou bring Him ten.

Oh joy for those who, when He sits upon His
  judgement throne,
Shall humbly bring unto their King the gifts
  He loves to own—
" Pieces of silver " pure, all stamped with His
  own Royal Seal,
Which He may store where never more shall
  thief break through and steal.

And they who win such jewels for His Crown
  and for His Shrine,
For evermore His Throne before as glorious stars
  shall shine,
Oh seize the silver while ye may, and brightly
  shall it gleam,
When staff in hand, at His command, ye go
  down to the stream !

The LORD of Life is with His own, His path is
  in the sea,
He guides them in their Exodus, His right hand
  sets them free ;
From wanderings sore, from pain and tears, into
  His own fair Fold—
CHRIST, of His mercy, bring us forth with silver
  and with gold !

Hymns

ADVENT

'TIS good, O JESU, that alone with Thee
    Thy servants in this solemn hour should
  be,
Alone on those dread verities to think
In sight of which our sinful spirits sink.
Death and the Judgement, Heaven, the awful
    Hell,
Grant us these four things to ponder well ;
Shun we the haunts of men — the festive
    tone ;
Rest we with Thee, O LORD, alone, alone.

For death is coming—first of those last things
To which we haste, borne on time's rapid
    wings.

Death with its fears, its weakness, and its pain,
With Satan's last attempt our soul to gain;
The thirst, the dark temptation to despair;
The dim bewilderment, the faltering prayer:
Oh, keep us in the hour of death Thine own,
When we, with Thee, shall be alone, alone.

After death the Judgement! Holy LORD,
Lest haply unto us the day be stored
With vengeance, let us now, on bended knee,
Muse on that dread, that dread reality—
The great White Throne, th' accusers manifold,
The Book whence thoughts, and words, and
        deeds are told;
When we with naught to plead, none to atone,
Shall stand before our Judge, alone, alone.

Hell—scarce we brook to syllable that name;
What if our endless portion be its flame!
Oh! bid us view it now, with weeping eyes,
The quenchless fire, the worm that never dies;
The groans, the mocking laughter, clanking
        chains,
Eternity of never-ceasing pains:
Cast out from GOD—all hope and joy are gone;
In midst of devils, yet alone, alone

And lastly Heaven—oh! how our hearts do
  burn,
Until the Sun of Righteousness return!
Musing on Heaven, we watch, and hope, and
  pray,
Until the dawning of that blessèd Day—
That bright eternal Day, which hath no night:
Thou its unfading Joy, its cloudless Light;
Dwelling with the FATHER and with HOLY
  GHOST,
The Crown and Prize of Thy Redeemèd Host.
                                    Amen.

LENT

AGAIN our Lent has come to us, the seed-
time of the year,
And we must late and early toil, that ere the
LORD appear,
Within the garden of our hearts such holy seed
be sown,
That every Fruit and every Flower the Gardener
may own.
The time is short—oh, labour all, with fast and
prayer and tear,
Because once more our Lent is come, the seed-
time of the year.

Cold are the winds of Nature now, and, oh! the
blasts are keen,
The searching blasts of deep remorse for what
our sins have been.

Soft are the showers that on the ground fall
    gently down from Heaven :
O JESU, to our cold hard hearts may penitence
    be given,
That we may sorrow unto Thee with many a
    secret tear,
Nor cast away the grace of Lent, the seed-time
    of the year.

Dig deep, O soul, the ground on which the
    winter's frost has lain,
That deep within the loving LORD may sow some
    seed again.
And, oh ! uproot each choking weed, e'en
    though their tendrils be
Twined closely round some earthly flower that
    is most dear to thee.
Cleanse well the soil—the time is short, the
    Sower draweth near,
And none dare waste the time of Lent, the seed-
    time of the year.

O Thou, the Eternal Word, the Seed and Sower
    of the Seed,
Turn not away from our poor hearts in their
    extremest need ;

But plant Thyself within us now, that in the
     last dread day,
When Thou, as Judge severe, each fruit shalt
     strictly sift and weigh—
Thou mayest own as Thine alone the "full corn
     in the ear,"
Sown and matured in these our Lents, the seed-
     time of the year.

                         Amen.

LENT

WE cry to Thee, O JESU,
    Ere yet the night-shades fall,
Ere yet the Bridegroom cometh,
    Ere yet we hear His call;
For Light, for Food, for Healing,
    Low at Thy Feet we fall.

We come for Light to Thee, LORD,
    Sole Day-spring, only Sun,
For long time in the darkness
    Our feet have wandered on;
Far from the narrow pathway
    Have wandered blindly on.

Oh! lighten Thou our darkness,
    We cannot find the way,
But farther still from Thee, LORD,
    Our wandering feet will stray;

Except Thy light shall lead us,
  Our wandering feet will stray.

We cry to Thee for Healing,
  Physician of the soul;
Though we be weak and wounded,
  Thy Hand can make us whole.
Oh! give our hearts contrition,
  And pitying make us whole.

For Food we come to Thee, LORD,
  Who art the Bread of Life,
Nought else can yield us courage
  To face the deadly strife.
Oh! strengthen us in mercy
  To conquer in the strife.

To Thee, the pure and sinless,
  Our feeble hymns of praise,
From lips so oft transgressing,
  Scarce dare we now to raise;
Oh! cleanse and make us meet, LORD,
  Thy Holy Name to praise.
                        Amen.

EASTER EVE

STILLNESS broods upon the earth,
  Calmed is sorrow, hushed is mirth,
Joy and gladness may not reign
Till the LORD has risen again.
In the pit our Joseph lies,
Cold His limbs, and closed His eyes,
And we, silent, watch and pray,
Till the dawn of Easter Day.

Grief and sorrow may endure
For a night, but joy is sure;
Joy entrancing soon shall come,
Joy to chase away our gloom.
Watching, waiting, let us pray,
Till the stone be rolled away,
Till we hear the Angel's voice :
"CHRIST is Risen! Rejoice, rejoice!"

'Tis a night to ponder well
In the tents of Israel,
'Tis the night that sets us free
From sin's dark captivity.
And we all, with lamp in hand,
Waiting for the Bridegroom stand,
With girt loins, and sandalled feet,
Prompt our Risen LORD to greet.

Alleluias soon shall rise
Pealing through the midnight skies.
To the strong man in his might
Came a stronger One this night,
Seized the spoils from out his hands,
Rent his prison, burst his bands:
Peace hath conquered sin and strife,
Death is swallowed up of Life.

Amen.

FIRST VESPERS OF EASTER AND OTHER GREAT FESTIVALS

AT Eventide was Light!
  When GOD creation framed,
The Day, in ordered course,
  He Eve and Morning named.

At Eventide is Light!
  Still in her holy round,
Evening and Morn the Church
  In one fair Feast hath bound

At Eventide is Light!
  With gladness all things shine;
We raise our songs of joy,
  We deck our altar-shrine.

131

At Eventide is Light!
  Yet watch we, lamp in hand,
And, waiting for our GOD,
  Within His House we stand!

At Eventide is Light!
  By Faith, by Hope, we see
Consummated, e'en now,
  To-morrow's mystery.

At Eventide be Light,
  When we our work have done!
Then look we for the Morn,
  That Morn without a sun!

When CHRIST shall lighten all
  In Heaven's Eternal Home.
Oh, come that blessèd Morn,
  E'en so, LORD JESU, come.
                    Amen.

S. GEORGE

LOUD in exultation
England's sons to-day
Fain to England's patron
Praise and honour pay.
Praising him they render
Worship to his LORD,
Whence alone all virtue
On His Saints is pour'd.

Sing we of his courage!
When his Master's Name
Evil men were loading
With contempt and shame,
He the Royal Edict
Dauntless flung aside,
Fearless e'en of dying,
As his LORD had died.

Sing we how believing,
  At Apollo's shrine
He, his LORD confessing,
  Made the holy sign!
Bade depart the demon
  Who the idol filled;
And the shattered image
  Showed his word fulfilled.

Sing we his endurance:
  Firm he bore his pain,
Glad by Martyr's torment
  Martyr's crown to gain;
Thankful that his Captain
  Gave to him a draught
Of that Cup of sorrows
  Which He once had quaffed.

Wide his fame resounded;
  Him—the lordliest knight,
Him—the lowest soldier
  Called on in the fight.
"Good S. George for England,"
  Was our battle-cry:
"Good S. George for England,"
  Brought us victory.

'Neath the red-cross banner
  Of the soldier-saint,
Who can fail or falter,
  And what heart can faint?
While it floats o'er England
  Calm be her repose;
Only be she faithful,
  GOD will quell her foes.

               Amen.

S. ALBAN

WE hail, renownèd Alban,
   With joy thy festal day;
For thou to England's children
   Hast ope'd a blessèd day.
First of her sons to enter
   By dint of mortal strife
Within the glorious portals
   Of everlasting life.

The first to win the palm-branch,
   The first to learn the song,
That glad new song, which only
   May chant the Martyr throng;
The first upon whose forehead
   Hath Angel-hand imprest
GOD's everlasting signet,
   The emblem of the blest.

Nor marvel we to see him,
   With such a world in sight,
Go down to death's dark river
   With joy and rapture bright:
Scarce marvel we that smiling
   Beneath the stream he sank,
For Heaven's light was shining
   Upon its further bank.

And on the blood-tracked pathway
   Where the young athlete led,
How many eager spirits
   Have pressed and thronged to tread!
Till " Isle of Saints " was England;
   And still her dearest boast
Is in her white-robed army,
   Her glorious martyr-host.

What though we be **not** callèd
   To die as Alban died,
Yet grant us, Holy JESUS,
   As Thou wast crucified,
In life and death to bear us
   As soldiers of the cross,
And count life's cherished pleasures
   Most cherished in their loss. Amen.

VISITATION OF S. MARY

DEEP thoughts were in her breast,
  As o'er the desert wild
The lonely Virgin pressed
  Who bore the Holy Child:
    And, fair as moon
      That rides the sky,
      In majesty
    She passeth on.

Bearing her GOD she goes,
  Oh! wonder passing thought!
Who may the awe disclose
  That in her spirit wrought?
    How silent fain
      With Him to meet
      In converse sweet
    She would remain.

But self no place may win.
　Upborne on wings of love,
Of virgins ever Queen,
　And Saint all Saints above,
　　She goes to bear
　　　Her holy part,
　　　With other heart
　　Her joy to share.

Grant us, O Ever Blest,
　From Mary's part to learn,
Not in earth's love to rest,
　Nor, proud, Heaven's gifts to spurn;
　　Our hearts keep free,
　　　And let them still,
　　　In good or ill,
　　Be stayed on Thee—

On Thee and on Thy love,
　To Whom all praise be paid—
By victor hosts above,
　By us for war arrayed;—
　　Till evermore,
　　　With angel throng,
　　　Th' unceasing song
　　We gladly pour.　Amen.

S. MARY MAGDALENE

LOVE and death have wrestled fiercely,
　　But to-day we raise on high
Heavenly song of glad thanksgiving;
　　Love hath triumphed gloriously.

Love hath bowed in deepest anguish
　　Head which once uplifted high
Sought for neither shrift nor blessing,
　　And hath triumphed gloriously.

See from Mary's eyes bent downward
　　Tears are flowing plenteously;
See, they bathe the Feet of JESUS;
　　Love hath triumphed gloriously.

See, that hair, once decked so richly,
　　Giv'n His sacred Feet to dry;

See the costly ointment pourèd;
   Love hath triumphed gloriously.

Love lays at His Feet most humbly
   Broken heart and bitter sigh,
All her treasures, all her pleasures;
   Love hath triumphed gloriously.

Now He gently lifts the fallen,
   Looks on her with pitying eye;
Love hath wrought a perfect pardon,
   And hath triumphed gloriously.

Praise the FATHER, praise the SPIRIT,
   Praise the SON, Who, GOD Most High,
Came to seek and save the helpless,
   And hath triumphed gloriously.
                      Amen.

S. PETER'S CHAINS

CALM the Saint's slumber—
  O tyrant, in vain
Guards in their number,
  The dungeon, the chain!
Gladly he weareth
  What JESUS hath worn,
Thankful he beareth
  What JESUS hath borne.

Vainly thou deemest,
  In pride of thy might,
That peril extremest
  The Saints shall affright.
Thou who would'st smite them
  With sword and with spear,
Know to requite them
  A Saviour is near.

Strong spells are working,
　The Church is at prayer,
Spirits are lurking
　Thou knowest not where;
See angels bringing
　Release to the prison,
Hear the Church singing,
　From terror uprisen.

His in the highest
　Be glory and power,
Who still is nighest
　In sorrow's dark hour;
Ever receiving,
　Blest Three and blest One,
Prayers which, believing,
　We lift to His throne.

　　　　　　　　　Amen.

S. FRIDESWIDE

A VIRGIN heart she brought to CHRIST,
   For Him she cast away
The passing glories of the world,
   The pomp of queenly sway—
All things save JESUS' love she spurned,
   Nor earthly spouse would know—
For Whom her soul loved she had found
   And would not let Him go.

As silver in the fire, was tried
   The Virgin's pure intent;
But dangers were as rest to her,
   And pain wrought sweet content—
Not one sharp pang, not one fierce word
   Would that brave heart forego—
For Whom her soul loved she had found
   And would not let Him go.

They hunted her from place to place,
    But JESUS by her side
Did wondrously to guard her faith
    And shield His spotless Bride.
Well might she all endure, whose LORD
    Was laid in manger low—
For Whom her soul loved she had found
    And would not let Him go.

At length GOD, pitying, gave her rest,
    In prayer that rest was found,
And where she dwelt is for her sake
    Revered as holy ground.
In Prayer, in Eucharist, in Hymn
    Her life was passed below,
For Whom her soul loved she had found
    And would not let Him go.

The love we laud, O JESUS blest,
    That nerved a Virgin frail
Such deeds to do, such pangs to bear,
    Nor in Thy sight to fail,—
Now in perfect Light of Heaven,
    While endless ages flow,
She holdeth Him Whom here she served,
    Nor e'er will let Him go.   Amen.

THE WORSHIP OF THE CHURCH

I LOVE the Courts of JESUS! but not be-
cause they're bright
With azure or with ruby, and forms all fair to
sight:
'Tis not the 'broidered vestment, and gems of
beauty rare,
Not gold and silver beaming that draw my foot-
steps there.
　　Though still mine eyes delight to trace
　　The beauty of that Holy Place;
　　To see earth's choicest gifts brought nigh
　　The LORD of all to glorify.

I love the Courts of JESUS! but not because
they're fraught
With recollections telling of what our fathers
wrought:

'Tis not that they for ages have heard the chants
    we raise ;
'Tis not because here prayèd good men of other
    days.
  But yet I love to feel we're one
  With days of faith and love now gone—
  To know our prayers are still addressed
  In fellowship with Saints at rest.

I love the Courts of JESUS ! but not because 'tis
    sweet
That voice with voice harmonious, and heart
    with heart should meet :
'Tis not that here our brethren are gathered
    with one mind
To seek our GOD, where surely all they who
    seek shall find.
  And yet 'tis joy that here on earth
  We antedate the heavenly mirth,
  Where day and night the endless song
  Like " many waters " they prolong.

I love the Courts of JESUS ! for angels " bright
    and fair "
Come down the golden ladder and mingle with
    us there :

They praises sing with fervour, where man per-
  chance is cold,—
Fall prostrate round the altar, than sinful man
  less bold.
    Then swiftly back by that same stair
    (Of CHRIST Incarnate symbol rare !)
    Our feeble praise and faltering prayer,
    As incense sweet on high they bear.

I love the Courts of JESUS ! for here His Name
  is set
To bless and cheer and strengthen where two
  or three are met ;
And most I love His Altar, where He that hath
  been slain
Renews Love's mighty Mystery to our unending
  gain.
    Oh well I love the House of GOD,
    By CHRIST indwelt, by angels trod ;
    And much I prize this gate of Heaven,
    Where CHRIST to man is freely given !
                                        Amen.

HYMN FOR SISTERS

"YE have not chosen Me," He saith,
  "But I have chosen you."
O wondrous Love, half-willing souls
  Unwearying to pursue.
O happy souls who hear that Voice,
  Nor drive the call away,
Responding, "My Beloved is mine,
  "And I am His for aye."

The world is bright, He made it so,
  Its flowers bloom fair and sweet,
But we must bravely onward press,
  Nor rest our weary feet.
'Tis joy to tread where CHRIST hath trod,
  Though strewn with thorns the way,
For surely "My Beloved is mine,
  "And I am His for aye."

Full gently on **our** ears the tones
   Of earthly love may fall,
But we can give them little heed
   When CHRIST is made our all.
In lowliness and thankfulness,
   We praise **Him** day by day,
Still answ'ring, " My Beloved is mine,
   " And I am His for aye."

And pain is sweet, and weakness strength,
   And scorn may well be prized,
Since He our Master and our King
   By man was once despised.
'Mid every grief that can befall,
   His love shall be our stay,
For surely " My Beloved is mine,
   " And I am His for aye."
                          Amen.

THE CAROL OF THE BELLS ON NEW YEAR'S EVE

ALLELUIA! Miserere!
  Hark the bells now rising, falling;
Miserere, Alleluia,
  Wanes the Old Year past recalling.

Miserere, Miserere,
  Spare us feeble, frail and sinning;
Alleluia, Alleluia,
  Bless the New Year now beginning.

Miserere, Miserere,
  Ring out bells of solemn warning;
Alleluia, Alleluia,
  Night but heralds in the morning.

De Profundis Miserere,
 Oh! the past year's dark transgressions;
Miserere, De Profundis,
 JESU, hear our meek confessions.

Miserere, Miserere,
 Ere the year be past forgive us;
Miserere, De Profundis,
 From our sins, oh! GOD, relieve us.

Alleluia, Alleluia,
 He hath spared, nought shall oppress us;
Alleluia, Alleluia,
 We are His and He will bless us.

Alleluia, Miserere,
 Still the midnight chimes are pealing;
Alleluia, Alleluia,
 Softly o'er the spirit stealing.

Gloria Deo in excelsis,
 Peace be here and holy gladness;
Alleluia, Alleluia,
 Hence with fear and gloom and sadness.

Miserere, Alleluia,
　Through the New Year let us measure,
As Eternity foreboding,
　Days and hours—our precious treasure!

Alleluia, Alleluia,
　Ring out clearly, ring out lightly;
Alleluia, Alleluia,
　Greet the New Year, greet it brightly.
　　　　　　　　　　Amen.

THE HOLY CROSS

MID the bitter waters Moses,
  Faithful, casts the sweetening tree
Isaac rears Moriah's altar,
  Th' offering himself to be;
Israel, by the serpents bitten,
  On the wood their healing see.

David's *Son has made his Chariot;
  Costly woods its frame supply,
Gold the floor, while silver pillars
  Bear its purple canopy—
Signs of love that JESUS lifted
  Through the Cross up to the sky.

O Jerusalem, that crownest
  Noblest sons with bitterest scorn,

* Solomon's Chariot (*Cant.* iii. 9) is reckoned among the types
of the *Cross.*

Couldst thou weave for thy Redeemer
   Only wreath of torturing thorn
In the day of His espousals,
   On that last and saddest morn?

But when He His Spirit yielded,
   See from forth His piercèd Side
Come (as Eve of old from Adam),
   Holy Church, His Spotless Bride—
On the Cross her life beginning,
   Grant her still there to abide.

Bind us to it, Holy JESU,
   Let us ever hold it fast,
Cling to it in sin and sorrow;
   And when life is well nigh passed,
Stretched upon its bosom, float us
   O'er death's stream to Thee at last—

Unto Thee, where high exalted,
   Thou, our worship, evermore
Standest; while the white-robed elders
   With the angel hosts adore,
And to Thee, with GOD the FATHER,
   And the SPIRIT, praises pour.
                  Amen.

Poems

ARCHBISHOP LAUD

TO one of old 'twas shown that for each land
    An Angel Prince as guardian e'er doth
    stand,
And if for countries, surely GOD hath given
To every Church an Angel Prince in Heaven;
Nor only Angels watch, but spirits blest
Of just men perfect made; and foremost placed
In that high rank are those who have embraced
Death for their LORD, and for their LORD'S dear
    Bride;
And, having lived for GOD, for GOD have
    died.
Now one there is amid the noble band
Of Martyrs gathered from our own dear
    land,

To whose blest name a grateful Church must
    cling :
The martyred servant of a martyred King—
He bore his part in times of troublous strife,
When heresy and wild revolt were rife ;
When men would fain old boundaries remove,
And England had forgotten her first love.
Then Laud uprose, and manfully he fought,
Straight at the fountain-head each truth he
    sought ;
To those old Fathers who CHRIST'S mind had
    learned
For dogma and interpretation turned ;
What men had lost from holy Creed or rite,
He faithfully brought forth again to light ;
What they had added, stern he cast aside
As a dishonour to the Church, CHRIST'S
    Bride.
Then men beheld 'neath Laud's restoring
    hand
The Church again in fair proportions stand ;
He knew to sever with unerring ken
'Twixt ancient truth and phantasies of men ;
And boldly to defend from Rome's designs
Our Church's Creed and England's glorious
    shrines ;

And he who thus built up the ancient faith,
And for its sake endured a Martyr's death,
Must still methinks (although he may **not** know
Perchance what passes in this world below)
Be praying oft before the throne on high
For that loved Church for which he dared **to** die.
He knows—as one inspired by GOD—that still
Will evil men 'gainst England's Church work
    ill;
And well doth he, the great Archbishop. know
The boon to ask in Heaven for us below.
Oh! may his ardent spirit brave and true,
And his friend's noble motto, " Through and
    through,"
Still rule our Pastors, that our Church may be
Full of all courage, faith, and loyalty—
A city fair set on GOD's Holy Hill,
And by His SPIRIT guarded from all ill.

ALL SOULS' DAY

BE still this day, no sound of mirth;
   Its darkness is beseeming—
This day beholds the ancient earth
   With ancient myriads teeming.

And all the air with voiceless prayer
   Is heavily o'erburdened,
For the cry and the groan of wild despair
   Hath GOD with silence guerdoned.

Remorse to-day, that ruthless king,
   Whose realm is hopeless grieving,
Hath power his fiercest pangs to bring,
   Nor GOD can give relieving.

"One moment only once again
   "Of my most lost probation,
"The time to breathe one true 'Amen!'"
   Oh, cry of desolation!

"The time to do one act of love
　"To the poor that GOD hath given,
"One act that would be owned above,
　" High in the holy Heaven."

Beside their " brethren five " they stand,
　Whom they would fain be telling
Some secrets of the silent land
　Wherein they have their dwelling.

But on their lips is a strange cold seal,
　And that seal may not be broken,
All they are yearning to reveal
　Must be for aye unspoken.

Oh, hush this day light sounds and gay,
　For the voiceless dead surround us;
Those who have lived and have passed away
　Are gathered here around us.

But who are those who glide around,
　And seek the Church's portal—
And give GOD thanks for battle crowned
　By the hope of life immortal?

They gather round each holy shrine,
  Where JESUS oft hath met them;
Those moments full of love divine,
  They never can forget them!

And in this hour with holy power,
  Their prayers to Heaven ascending,
Rise up a strong and mighty tower,
  With the prayers of JESUS blending.

Oh, it may be perchance that we,
  Ere another year is breaking,
Among the dead shall gathered be
  Till the everlasting waking.

Kneel, kneel and pray while thy soul may
  To the SAVIOUR Who will hear thee:
    "LORD, in my death's most fearful hour,
    "Guard me, O guard from the tempter's
      power,
" And in Thine awful Judgment Day,
" Oh, let my place be near Thee."

M

CHRIST IN THE TEMPLE

LORD JESUS ! much we ponder when we read
　　Of that strange scene within the temple
　　　bound ;
Left with the sinner in her sorest need,
　　Thou stooping down didst write upon the
　　　ground.
Of old they wrote Thy heavy curse on guilt,
　　Then sacred dust and holy water took—
That water on the accusing record spilt—
　　Blotted it out for ever from the Book.
LORD, may we dare to think that from Thine
　　　eyes,
　　To cleanse her sin, a holier water flowed?
Out of the dust our contrite prayers arise,
　　That Thou wouldst turn from us th' avenging
　　　rod,
And all our sins and our iniquities
　　Wash out for ever, blessed tears of GOD !

INTERCESSIONS

GO where we will, we cannot flee from prayer;
It walls us in although we know it not;
From busy town, and field, and desert spot,
The mighty voice goes up and fills the air.

The weary watcher, on his bed of pain,
Brings down a blessing on another's health;
The poor man sanctifies his neighbours'
wealth,
And what he gives, GOD gives to him again.

And not alone our cries of anguish seek
Him Who has made our bitterest griefs His
own;
But with the prayers of faithful souls and meek
Rising in countless crowds to the great
throne:
Thus fenced with strength, albeit poor and weak,
Go where we will, we cannot be alone.

THE MYSTIC ARK

AS in mystic ark was stored
Threefold witness of the LORD—
Rod that Aaron's priesthood sealed,
Law on Sinai's mount revealed,
Manna Israel that sustained
Till the land of rest they gained—
So, LORD, in our spirits frail
May this order aye prevail:
Be Thy law within our heart
Graven deep in every part;
There implant Thy Cross divine,
Not in dry and lifeless sign,
Striking far and firm its root,
Bright with blossom, rich in fruit;
Be Thy sacramental Food
Source of full beatitude,
All our life as now we press
Onward through the wilderness.

In its power with Thee we tread
Where Thy bleeding Feet have led;
We the mournful way retrace,
Thorn and shame with Thee embrace
In that Food's sustaining strength;
On the Mount of GOD at length,
We the unveiled Majesty
Of our King unscathed shall see.
Gold within and gold without
Overlaid that ark about,
Figuring to us that we
Must be clothed in charity.
Love to Thee within shall glow,
Love to man must overflow,
In a tender, watchful care,
Loads to lighten, griefs to share.
Thus, O LORD, life's source and fount,
By the pattern in the Mount,
Grant us all our lives to frame
To the glory of Thy Name.

AN OLD LEGEND

A MAN of old, when death drew near,
   Beheld as in a dream
A Judgement, and the scales wherein
   An Archangel did seem
To weigh his good and evil deeds—
   The good rose to the beam.

Then cried he, weeping, "Oh, my GOD,
   "Will nothing here prevail?
"Will all Thy painful Passion now
   "For me have no avail?"
Into the scale of good there fell
   Anon a heavy Nail.

And the good deeds outweighed the rest,
   The bad went up apace;

It was a Nail from JESUS' Hand,
  And bore full many a trace
Of a wound whence one sole drop might well
  Bring endless peace and grace.

Next morn before the Altar-throne
  The old man lowly bent,
A smile of joy was on his face
  And the sun his glory lent
To the tabernacle of a soul
  Whose veil should soon be rent.

The light shone round the shaven head
  Through many a tinted pane;
He knelt to receive the Angels' Food,
  And he rose not up again.
For CHRIST the LORD in Heaven had claimed
  A soul He had died to gain.

Page 169

PAST the range of Satan's dart,
    Nearer than my fretful heart,
Far beneath and far above,
Is my Saviour's faithful love.

More mine own than mind and frame,
Older than my sin and shame,
More my life than blood or breath,
Deeper than the pits of death.

Though I altogether fail
None can reach Thee, or assail;
Still to Thee I turn my face,
Still unconquered is Thy grace.

When desire or memory
Rise to hold me back from Thee,
When the chambers of the brain
Echo voices fierce or vain,

Still the faith Thou gavest own,
Grant the prayer, nor heed the groan;
Bind Thou my rebellious feet,
I abandon all retreat.

While the vanities decay,
Till the anger pass away,
Through the dying storm's lament,
In Thy will I lie content.

P. N. W., S.S.J.E.

"BE COMFORTED"

"BE comforted, O child of My delight,
    "Though yet thy heart complain ;
"For I would have thee suffer while I smite,
    "Or pain would not be pain.

"And who is he who seeks the haven fair,
    "The everlasting Home?
"The lonely and the outcast enter there,
    "The glad heart will not come.

"To Me the weary cometh when the way
    "Is steep and long and lone ;
"To Me the friendless, when the golden day
    "Behind the hills is gone."

MAGDALEN AT MICHAEL'S GATE

MAGDALEN at Michael's gate tirled at
the pin;
The blackbird sang on Joseph's thorn,
" Let her in, let her in."

" Hast thou seen the Wounds," said Michael,
and knowest thou thy sin?"
"'Tis evening, 'tis evening," sang the black-
bird;
" Let her in, let her in."

" Yes, I have seen the Wounds," she said, " and
I know my sin."
" She knows it well, well, well," sang the
blackbird;
" Let her in, let her in."

When he had sung himself to sleep, and night
    did begin,
ONE came and opened Michael's gate—
    And Magdalen went in.

              Henry Kingsley
                (by permission).

A CHRISTMAS GIFT

" PRAY that your flight be not in wintry
   weather ! "
So has He warned us, tender for all other ;
Yet it was winter when they fled together,
   He and His Mother !

" Trees of the woodland, give now your fuel,
" That warmth and comfort His sweet life may
   cherish ;
" Else in the midnight dark and cold and cruel
  " My Son will perish ! "

Answered the ash : " My branches grow too
   greenly,
" Less fit to kindle than to quench a fire ;
" Yet to give all is not to offer meanly—
  " Have thy desire."

Answered the hazel: "Though no more I
   flourish,
"Though leaf and blossom fail the copse to
   gladden,
"If the world's Saviour thus my death might
   nourish,
      "I should not sadden!"

Therefore the hazel bears her catkin token,
Long ere the chilly winter has departed:
Therefore the ashwood burns when freshly
   broken,
      Ever warmhearted.

M. A. Yonge.

O JESU, Rest upon the road;
  O JESU, Shadow by the way;
O JESU, Who dost light the load
  Of tired toilers all the day.

O grateful Coolness in the heat;
  O Fount that never knowest fail;
O pleasant Rest for weary feet:
  O Lamb of GOD, O Holy Grail.

(Attributed to A. G. E. W.)

Printed by A. R. Mowbray & Co. Ltd., London and Oxford